# Reflections of Hope

Terry Lotus

# Contents

Reflections of Hope



ISBN-13: 979-8-8692-5693-5 (softcover)

ISBN-13: 979-8-8692-5694-2 (e-book)

Stock or custom editions may be purchased in bulk for educational, business, ministry, fundraising, or sales promotional use.

# Preface

Most of my life has been spent in turmoil fashioned by a desperate need to love and be loved. A childhood filled with emotional neglect, betrayal, and child sexual abuse etched the roadmap of my life of desperation. This desperation led to poor choices, some of which came at a very high price. You will read about things I've done that have given me great joy, as well as things for which I have deep regret. You will also read about my spiritual journey that began with a belief in God, led to a rejection of God, and came full circle back home to the Lord Jesus Christ.

I share my story as a way to provide hope to those who have floundered through life as I did, destined to repeat the same pattern - destined to repeat the same mistakes. Each chapter is followed by a Reflection of Hope and Scriptures of Hope that I pray will enlighten you and inspire you to change the course of your life - to find peace.

The names of the people mentioned in this book have been changed to preserve their anonymity. The names aren't important; the messages are. I don't share these experiences to generate shock and awe but in hope that if you are headed down a similar path to what I followed, you will find the strength and courage to begin to walk a different road - a road where you can find your true self. Never give up and never lose hope. God bless.

# Chapter 1

## *The Beginning of the End*

*For he will command his angels concerning you to guard you in all your ways.*

— Psalm 91:11 ESV

"Mommy in hospital and can't feel good." I found these words in my baby book in my dad's handwriting.

The complete entry is, "What a sad summer. You were 2 years and 4 mo old when your mommy passed away. You had been to the hospital to see her and were old enough to realize that as you said, 'Mommy in hospital and can't feel better.' No need to try to explain, as you are much too little to comprehend. But some day when you are older, I will tell you the sad story. August 13, 1961. Your loving dad."

My mother died on July 23, 1961, of a pulmonary embolism while undergoing a hysterectomy at the age of thirty-seven.

My mom and dad married on October 17, 1958, a little over five months before I was born. I have no memory of my mother, only a few tattered black-and-white photos. One of the photos is of the two of us outside on a cold winter day, where she was holding me tightly in her arms. She was beaming. She had dressed me for the weather in a heavy wool coat, mittens, and a white knit hat that had ties hanging from the ear flaps and a small yarn ball on the top. In another photo, my mother is sitting on the corner of a picnic table in a park, wearing a white skirt suit with white gloves in hand. On the bench next to her is a straw purse with pictures of dogs on the front of it. Again, she is beaming.

My baby book contains entries in both my dad's and what I assume is my mother's handwriting. There are many first-year entries in my baby book, including when I began to "creep," one noting I received a stuffed horse and a dog on my first Christmas, the day I spoke my first word, which was "down," and a list of presents I received on my first birthday. There are only two second-year entries in my baby book; one of the entries I mentioned earlier and the second entry was, "Noticed the stars for the first time. Nov. 3, 1961, 8:00 p.m." Entries on the third-year pages included, "Daddy baked a two-layer black walnut cake, what a time with the frosting, but I made it." and "You got up this A.M. and put white shoe polish all over the television glass, and all over the black controls. What a mess." At this point, my dad was raising me on his own and continued to make entries in my baby book. I have only one memory of my dad after my mother died. He was taking me to daycare early in the morning. My small hand was securely grasped by his, which gave me a sense of comfort and security. I was wearing long pants, a warm coat, mittens, and a knit hat. My dad greeted the daycare ladies with his friendly smile and sent me off with a hug.

There are no entries in my baby book after the third year, which comes as no surprise, as I was four years old when my dad married my stepmother, Brenda, and my world was turned upside-down.

## A World Unraveled

Brenda was a widow with two sons when she married my dad. At the time, her son Brandon was ten years old, and George was seventeen. I can't help but think it was a marriage of convenience, as I never witnessed any affection between my dad and Brenda. When I told my half-sister this, she said, "That's not what you did in those days. You never showed any affection in front of anyone else." Okay, I can buy that, but this went beyond "That's not what you did in those days." At home, my dad and Brenda were almost robotic with each other. Each performed their role as wife and man of the house, but there were no conversations between them beyond those of necessity, and after a few years, Brenda's bed became the living room couch.

When my dad married Brenda, he went from being a dad who baked two-layer black walnut cakes with me to a dad who was disconnected and remained in the background. He was disconnected from the boys as well, especially from George, for reasons I wouldn't understand until later.

Brenda would constantly dote over Brandon and George but was void of affection for me. I was more of an obligation to her. While Brenda was taking milk and homemade cookies to the boys when they went to bed, I went to bed alone and in silence.

We moved into an older brick house in a middle-class neighborhood. The backyard was fenced, and there was an incinerator adjacent to the alleyway. One winter, it snowed so heavily we couldn't open the side door of the house to go outside. Six-foot drifts of snow settled against the fence and incinerator. Brandon and I spent the afternoon digging out the center of two drifts, creating forts that provided shelter during snowball battles.

In the front room, there was a large picture window. If the curtains were left open, birds would fly into the window, not realizing it was there, and fall to the ground, lifeless. I was horrified and overwhelmed with sadness the first time I witnessed this. From that day forward, I made it my job to make sure the sheer curtains were drawn at all times to ensure there would be no more head-on collisions with the window.

I had my own bedroom on the main floor of the house, next to the master bedroom. The boys shared a bedroom in the attic. The wooden staircase leading to the attic was narrow and twisted. The bedroom was long and the a-frame ceiling and walls were covered with wood paneling. Two single beds were nestled against opposite walls.

In the basement was a well-stocked bar spread out along the back wall. My dad's heavy metal desk was in a corner, and he was sure to have a bottle of bourbon in the bottom right-hand drawer. My kitchen play set shared a corner with the furnace.

Superficially, Brenda was a model wife and mother. While working full-time, Brenda kept the house spotless, washed and ironed our clothes, and even ironed the pillowcases. She made all of our well-rounded meals from scratch; nothing she cooked or baked ever came from a box. Brenda always dressed well, never forgetting the matching accessories, and she made sure the boys and I also dressed well, especially on Sundays when the world would be watching. Brenda was proper in everything she did, from how she spoke and carried herself to how she would entertain guests in our home. To Brenda, appearances were everything.

My dad was a tall man with a solid build. He was a hard worker, God-fearing, very social, and was always heavily involved in organizations whose mission was to help the underprivileged. My dad and Brenda were very different in one important way; to the outside world, there was never any pretense when it came to my dad. Brenda, on the other hand, was all about pretense.

Life in our house was very scripted. During the week, my dad and Brenda went to work as the boys and I set off to school. At the end of the day, my dad would come home and head straight to the basement to "work" at his desk and sip bourbon until he was called to dinner. Brenda would come home from work, change out of her work clothes, tie an apron neatly around her waist, and prepare dinner while nursing a glass of wine. Around six o'clock in the evening, Brenda would call us all to dinner. She was a good cook, so we would all wait in anticipation of hearing her shout to everyone, "Dinner's ready." We would assemble at the kitchen table, on which there were five properly placed settings and a mouthwatering meal, properly served.

There were no conversations during dinner. No one asked how school was or how our day went. My dad and Brenda might say a few words to each other, but mostly we ate in silence. When my dad finished his dinner, he would leave the table and his dirty dishes and go downstairs to watch television. The boys followed suit, leaving their dirty dishes on the table as they ran off to their room. When I was older, I would help Brenda clear the table and do the dishes. My job was to dry the dishes with a dish towel as she rinsed them and placed them in the sink. As with dinner, this kitchen-cleaning ritual was conducted with very few or no words spoken between us.

## Betrayal at the Creek

In our neighborhood, I never had friends my age that I could play with. I would try to tag along or include myself in the games the older kids played, but would quickly be left behind. As I grew older, Brandon would let me hang out with him in his bedroom and listen to albums. I liked the cool posters of his favorite bands he had taped to the walls and wished I was old enough to have albums and hang posters on my bedroom walls. Brandon was the only one in the family who paid any attention to me, and I soaked it up like a sponge.

A favorite neighborhood place to play in the summertime was down by the creek, about a quarter of a mile from our house. Thick brush and tall trees bordered the creek on one side. Winding through the brush were paths that the children had made over the years. A tire, tied to a rope, hung from a tree branch that reached over the creek. Kids who were brave enough would swing on the tire and release themselves as the tire reached its highest point over the water.

On one particularly hot summer day, a boy swimming in the creek emerged from the water screaming. I looked over to see what was happening and saw the boy standing in the creek, paralyzed with fright, muddy water dripping from his hair, and bloodsuckers covering his torso. I never went in the creek, nor swung on the tire swing.

The only time I was allowed to go to the creek was when I was with Brandon. We would walk the quarter mile to the creek and I would sit on the bank and watch the kids playing in the water while Brandon went off with his friends. Being a girl, and only seven years old, Brandon, who was thirteen, didn't want his little sister hanging around with him and his teenage friends. After a while, he would come and pick me up, and we would head back to the house.

One day when Brandon and I went to the creek, he didn't drop me off to sit on the bank, but led me into the thick brush. I thought this was a little strange and asked him where we were going.

He answered, "Just follow me."

I trusted Brandon and was more than willing to go on an adventure with him. We walked along the path for a few minutes. It was like a wonderland. The thick brush above me blocked the hot summer sun, and the dirt felt cool beneath my bare feet. As we were walking, the path opened up into a small clearing. Brandon stopped suddenly and turned around to face me. You couldn't see anyone through the thicket, but you could hear the kids laughing and playing in the creek. I stopped and asked Brandon what we were doing there. Brandon asked me if I would take off all of my clothes so that he could look at me. I was stunned and confused at the request.

*I don't understand. I can't believe he wants me to take off my clothes and look at me. That is so wrong. I'm his sister! I don't want to take off my clothes in front of him and let him look at me. What if someone sees us? I don't want to do this!*

My heart began to race and I told him I wanted to leave. Brandon became a little nervous and said, "If you take off all of your clothes and let me look at you, I will let you hang out with me and my friends."

You'd think I would have immediately turned and ran out of the thicket, but I didn't. I was torn between feeling humiliated and being accepted as part of Brandon's group, if only by association. For the first time in my life, I realized how void of love and a sense of belonging my life was and how much I longed for friendship and attention. Humiliation seemed like a fair price, so I reluctantly agreed to the bargain.

With tears streaming down my face, I took off my pink cotton shorts, folded them, and gingerly laid them on the ground beside my feet. Next, I took off my white, short-sleeved shirt, folded it, and lightly placed it on my shorts, hoping to minimize any soiling. I stood there momentarily as if I was finished, hoping this would be enough, but this just made Brandon more nervous.

"Hurry, take off your underwear and turn around," he commanded.

I quickly removed my white cotton underwear and placed it on top of the pile. I closed my eyes, so I wouldn't see him looking at me, and quickly turned around, wanting it to be over as soon as possible.

*Why did I do this? I feel dirty and so ashamed. I should have run away. I don't ever want to see him again. How could a brother do this to his sister? I can't believe I'm doing this. I'm so embarrassed. I'm a bad girl.*

When I opened my eyes, Brandon had already started down the path to exit the thicket. I quickly put my clothes back on, wiped the tears from my face, and began to slowly walk down the path behind him. When I cleared the thicket, Brandon was gone; I was relieved. I didn't want to see him, much less play with him and his friends. The price had been too high.

I began the long walk home alone, brushing the dirt off of my pink shorts. I replayed the scene in my mind, over and over again, not wanting to believe it really happened. I felt betrayed by the only person who showed a sliver of love for me. I remembered the boy who emerged from the creek covered with bloodsuckers and thought I would gladly trade places with him right now. That was the last time I went to the creek or trusted anyone until I met Eileen.

## God Sent Me an Angel

Eileen was about nineteen years old and lived with her mother in a small white house across the street and three houses over. She was tall and thin with long, blonde hair and was kind of plain-looking. Eileen was an earthy girl who would blow her nose using a large maple leaf instead of a tissue. The first time I saw her do this, it made me laugh. She looked at me and brushed it off as if to say, "Why not?" I can't remember how I came to know Eileen, but she soon became my special friend.

I remember taking long walks together on warm summer days, talking and listening to one another with interest in what the other had to say. On one of our walks, we happened upon a small wooden house that had been converted into a record store. I'd never been in a record store before and was instantly amazed at the abundance of record albums neatly arranged in open-ended cubbies so that one could flip through the upright stacks and make a selection.

I was mesmerized by the array of colorful posters, jewelry, and glass formations on display on shelves and inside large glass cabinets. The smell of patchouli oil and burning incense in the "hippie" atmosphere made me feel right at home. I began to mimic the shoppers by flipping through the record albums as I listened to the rock-n-roll music playing throughout the small store. I felt the expanse of the world of music opening up to me as I realized the vastness of different artists and genres of music.

As I looked through the albums, I recognized one I had seen in Brandon's bedroom, which reminded me of the times Brandon and I would hang out in his room and listen to his albums. This fond memory was soon shattered by the memory of the humiliating betrayal I felt as I stood naked in front of Brandon in the thicket by the creek.

"Are you ready to go?" Eileen asked, as she gently placed her hand on my shoulder.

"Yup," I replied, feeling grateful for the interruption.

Eileen led me to the checkout counter where she purchased an album. When we were outside the store, Eileen gave me the album. I took the album from her and looked at her with great confusion. She told me she bought the album for me. I could hardly believe it. And so began the whirlwind of thoughts spinning around in my head. *Eileen bought this for me? It's too much. Can I accept it? I really want to accept it. I've never had an album before. Oh my gosh, I can't believe this is happening.*

I looked down at the album and saw it was Bridge Over Troubled Water by Simon and Garfunkel. I wasn't familiar with this music, but somehow it seemed perfect. I thanked Eileen and gave her a big hug. I felt so very special and loved. Brandon made me feel something similar at first, but feeling it from Eileen made me realize Brandon's attention wasn't love; it was something else entirely. I knew what I was feeling at that moment was pure, unselfish love for me, and I knew I loved Eileen.

I snuck the album in the house and hid it in my bedroom. I knew Brenda wouldn't let me keep it. On the rare occasion when no one else was home, I would sneak up to Brandon's room and play the album on his stereo. I was right. It *was* perfect.

One day when I was at Eileen's house, we were making candy and she gave me a book called The *Secret Garden*. On one of the first pages, Eileen had written a full-page inscription. It was written in cursive, so I couldn't read most of it, but I could read "Love always, Eileen" at the bottom. Again, I felt Eileen's pure love for me—the kind of love where you give and expect nothing in return. My heart was bursting with love for her, and again, I gave her a big hug of gratitude.

I still have the book Eileen gave me, and over the years, I will sometimes read the inscription, which always leaves me with tears streaming down my cheeks. "To Terry, The girl I will always love. Always remember that sensitivity is not a fault, try not to build a wall around your feelings, they are often the most valuable things you can give to another person. You will be hurt sometimes - but more often you will gain treasured friends. Remember that small things are often the most important. Learn all that you can about everything. Pray that you will have the courage to change the things you can change. The strength to accept the things you cannot change - and the wisdom to know the difference. Terry, you are only one person, but you are one. You can't do everything - but there is much that you can do. As you grow older you will have much to offer other people. Remember, you have the ability to become anything that you really want to become. Love Always, Eileen."

I told a friend about Eileen, who suggested I try to find her. What a wonderful idea! My Internet search returned pictures of various images, one of which I recognized as an older version of Eileen. The photo was linked to an obituary, which I read and knew it was describing my Eileen. An email for Eileen's brother was provided in the obituary, so I contacted him and told him how I knew his sister and asked him to confirm she was the Eileen I knew. He responded, "Yes, you have found her." He invited me to contact him to learn more about his sister.

During my two-hour conversation with Eileen's brother, I became steadfast in my belief that God had sent me an angel that very lovingly altered the course of my life. He told me Eileen received a degree in Exceptional Education, which she acquired to work with children with disabilities. He also said Eileen was deeply spiritual, and at about age 45, she moved to Safed, Israel, where she studied at a yeshiva for the last 25 years of her life and where she guided 12 - 18 mile walks in the wadi to Mt. Meron, the Sea of Galilee, and the Jordan River.

Shortly after Eileen gave me the book, we moved to Colorado and I would never see her again. That was a sad day for me, as Eileen made me look at the world with wonder and consider the possibilities. She restored my trust in people and showed me what genuine love is at a time when I associated love with betrayal. God truly sent me an angel to walk with me, if even for a short time.

## Reflection of Hope

I can't escape the feeling that I felt loved by my mother and dad when my mother was alive. I can feel this love as I read the entries in my baby book or look at the photo of me in my mother's arms. When my dad married Brenda, that love line was abruptly cut off and I was left to fend for myself. I often wonder what my life would have been like and who I would have become had my mother not died. I'm certain my life would have been very different, as I would have made choices from a love-filled heart instead of from an empty one.

Brandon was the only example of "love" I had experienced; at least I interpreted the attention he gave me to be love. I certainly hadn't experienced love from my dad or Brenda. In the thicket, by the creek, Brandon turned love and trust into humiliation and betrayal, leaving me ashamed and feeling undeserving of love.

I was raised in the Lutheran church, so I knew who God was and that He loved me, but the abandonment of love I experienced when my dad married Brenda made me begin to question my belief in God. He was supposed to love me and protect me. Where had he gone? Why did he take my mother from me? Why didn't he protect me from Brandon's violation? I felt He had abandoned me and I was left completely alone and shattered.

So often we question God's love for us. We wonder why he allows bad things to happen to us or to others we love. We drive ourselves crazy wondering why God didn't pay the rent this month or why He didn't prevent cancer from taking our loved one. But, nowhere in the Bible does God say, " I promise you will live a carefree life," so why do we go through life as if we are entitled to one and thinking God didn't keep His end of the bargain? We conveniently use God as a scapegoat for our misfortune and suffering and condemn Him, shaking our fist at the heavens.

In our fury, we forget about the promises God did make to us. The promises to love us, help us, and never leave us. God kept his promise by sending an angel to help me, to strengthen me, and to let me know He would be with me every step of the way. Through Eileen's loving kindness, God lifted me up, gave me a sense of worth, and restored my faith in love. Keep your eyes and heart open, so you can recognize an angel when God sends one your way, and know, God put his angels in charge of you to protect you wherever you go (Psalm 91:11 GNT).

## Scriptures of Hope

✝ God is always walking with us and will never abandon us. (Hebrews 13:5 GNT)

✝ For he shall give his angels charge over thee, to keep thee in all thy ways. (Psalms 91:11 KJV)

✝ But you, oh Lord, are a shield about me, my glory, and the lifter of my head. I cried aloud to the Lord, and He answered me from his Holy hill. (Psalms 3:3 ESV)

✝ The eternal God is your refuge, and his everlasting arms are under you. He drives out the enemy before you; he cries out, 'Destroy them!' (Deuteronomy 33:27 NLT)

✝ But the Lord is faithful; He will strengthen and guard you from the evil one. (II Thessalonians 3:3 CSB)

✝ Fear not, for I am with you; Be not dismayed, for I am your God. I will strengthen you, Yes, I will help you, I will uphold you with My righteous right hand." (Isaiah 41:10 NKJV)

✝ The Lord your God is in your midst, a mighty one who will save; he will rejoice over you with gladness; he will quiet you by his love; he will exult over you with loud singing. (Zephaniah 3:17 ESV)

✝ But you, O Lord, are a God of compassion and mercy, slow

to get angry and filled with unfailing love and faithfulness. (Psalms 86:15 NLT)

✝ Thank God, who did it all! His love never quits! (Psalms 136:26 MSG)

✝ For I know the plans I have for you, declares the LORD, plans for welfare and not for evil, to give you a future and a hope. (Jeremiah 29:11 ESV)

# Chapter 2

## *Love and Death*

*"Only love and death will change all things."*

— Kahlil Gibran

When I was eight years old we moved from Wisconsin to Colorado. Moving to Colorado softened the strain between Brandon and me, as our focus was drawn to the unknown. Brandon never apologized to me, and we never spoke about what happened; we had avoided one another and had barely spoken. But sharing an experience like moving to another state when you're eight and thirteen years old was enough to silently compel us to join forces. There was no formal pact, no pinky swear or spit-in-the-hand-and-shake gesture. It was a silent agreement, but the stipulations were understood.

For the most part, Brandon and I went back to a brother and sister relationship, but this time things were different, as Eileen had given me a sense of self-worth and the courage to stand against any threat to diminish it. I think Brandon sensed my newfound strength and respected it, which renewed the bond between us and made it even stronger.

Our first house in Colorado was located on a corner lot in a nice middle-class neighborhood. It was the smallest house on the street, surrounded mostly by old mansions. The house across the street was a large, two-story brick house with a huge lawn adjacent to it. An older couple lived there who didn't mind the neighborhood children claiming the lawn as their own for daytime play. Unlike the old neighborhood, there were a few children my age with whom I would play.

About seven blocks from our house was a school with a gigantic empty lot behind it. Brandon and I would walk to the lot and light off Estes rockets he had built from a kit. During the summer, there were craft-making classes at the school where my friends and I made braided bracelets out of colorful plastic strips and popsicle-stick houses that we could paint any color we wanted. I remember taking my works of art home and proudly showing them to Brenda, only to receive an indifferent "Uh huh."

Family life didn't change much when we moved, except that Brenda began to complain to me about my dad drinking. She would make remarks like, "He brought home a six-pack of beer." or "He's drunk again tonight." Until Brenda began to complain disapprovingly about my dad drinking, I had no idea it was a bad thing. I had always known my dad to drink, but I never saw a problem with it, as there was no stumbling, slurring of words, or passing out. I was surprised the first time Brenda confided in me about my dad drinking. Brenda never spoke to me about how she was feeling. It was remarkable to me and I interpreted it as attention and a relationship.

To maintain the wanted relationship, I began to side with Brenda and came to believe my dad was an alcoholic. One evening, Brenda and I were in the kitchen and she was ranting about my dad drinking and told me to tell him to stop drinking. I rarely spoke with my dad, so the thought of telling my dad to stop drinking was terrifying.

*I'm just a kid. I can't tell my dad to do anything. I can't believe Brenda would ask me to do this. I'm afraid of my dad's reaction. I won't do it. If you don't, you will ruin the relationship with Brenda. I can't do that. I've been wanting her attention for so long, and now that I have it, I don't want to lose it. Okay, I'll do it. I'm afraid.*

My dad walked into the kitchen a few minutes later and began talking with Brenda, who looked at me with prompting eyes as if to say, "Go ahead and tell him now." I took a deep breath and said, "Dad, will you stop drinking?" My dad looked at me perplexed, dropped his head slightly, and left the room without saying a word. I could see Brenda was happy with me, which made me feel aligned with her and worth any humiliation I may have caused my dad. The request to my dad to stop drinking didn't help the situation; it only aggravated it. His drinking increased, and so did Brenda's complaining. I felt bad about saying that to my dad, but it had made Brenda and I allies to some degree, which made it all worth it.

Brenda worked as a bookkeeper for the Lutheran church, and my dad was a salesman for a school supply company. George joined the military and Brandon and I continued to attend parochial school. I attended a Lutheran school attached to the church we went to every Sunday. The curriculum included a daily bible study class, and on Wednesdays, we would attend a short church service before lunch. This school was much more rigid than the school I attended in Wisconsin. Everything was very orderly and heavy-laden with rules and judgment. One of the punishments for breaking a rule included a paddling with a paddleboard the size of a ping pong paddle that had holes drilled in it to cut down the wind resistance on its way to our bare butts.

I had only one real friend during the three years I attended this school, and I didn't meet her until my last year. Her name was Charlotte and she was the only black student who had attended the school. She was in my class and no one would talk or play with her during recess. One day during recess, I asked Charlotte if she wanted to swing on the swings. Her face lit up, and she excitedly accepted my invitation. From that day forward, Charlotte and I played together every day during recess and soon became best friends.

That was the first time I experienced prejudice, and at the time, I didn't even know I had. After making friends with Charlotte, the students who used to talk with me in the halls or during recess, suddenly stopped associating with me. It took me a while, but I finally realized the other students didn't like Charlotte because she was black and didn't like me because I was her friend. Charlotte and I never talked about the fact that she had darker skin than I had or that none of the other kids wanted to be her friend because of it. We embraced the difference between us and built a friendship on it; one I will never forget.

## George Was Creepy

Brenda and George had an extremely codependent relationship that only subsided when George got married in his late forties, and his wife took over the mommy role. I wouldn't understand until much later in life the reasons why my dad felt such disdain toward George. It wasn't until recently that I learned from my half-sister that my dad didn't want George to move to Colorado with us. I'm sure my dad resented Brenda's coddling over George and wanted to sever, at least geographically, their co-dependent relationship. I'm sure this was a point of contention between my dad and Brenda and was a fight Brenda won.

Throughout his adult life, George acted childlike. And except for holding down a full-time job, George was lazy and expected his mother to take care of him and pay his way. This was another thing about George that didn't sit well with my dad, being a hard-working, self-sufficient, pay-your-own-way kind of guy. My dad hated the way George would always disappear when it came time to pay the check at a restaurant, or anywhere else, for that matter. I wonder if George ever had to pay rent or utilities or buy groceries all those years he lived with us. I would venture to guess George paid next to nothing, if anything, to contribute to his room and board, and this stuck in my dad's craw.

I shared in my dad's disdain of George, but for my own reasons; George was creepy. George did two things that would completely creep me out. For one, he would lecherously invade my bubble, and another thing, if that weren't enough, is he would publicly self-stimulate in close proximity to his testicles. Looking back, I realize George probably was suffering from a disorder of some sort, but from the perspective of a ten-year-old who had been manipulated into standing naked in front of her step-brother, George was creepy. I did my best to avoid him and would rarely talk with him, which also seemed to be Brandon's relationship with George.

Our family was fragmented within itself and within each of us, never connecting in a healthy way. No trips to the park or the ice cream shop. No pushes on swings or bedtime stories. No hugs. No kisses. No "I love you" or "You did a great job." Only fragmentation.

## Fading Away

I was eleven years old the third and last year I attended the Lutheran school. It was the year I met my best friend Charlotte and was also the year that the landscape of my life shifted. One day, as I was going down the stairs to go outside for recess, I felt a warm gush of something running down my legs. I stopped and looked down to see what it was and became terrified as I watched my socks absorb the blood. I began to scream, and soon the eyes of the other students were all focused on me; their faces overcome with a look of horror. A female teacher came up to me and led me to the bathroom. She helped me get cleaned up and gave me a feminine napkin to use. She was very kind and explained what was happening to me.

I was bewildered and didn't fully comprehend what she was telling me, but I understood the part about this only happening to girls. I began to think... *Brenda used to be a girl and had to know about this. Why didn't she tell me about this? I'm so embarrassed. What is going to happen when I leave the school today? Will everyone laugh at me and make fun of me? I can't come back to school after this. I hate Brenda for not telling me about this.*

Dad picked me up from school and we drove home in silence. When we got home, I immediately went to my bedroom and didn't come out until it was dinner time. About an hour after Brenda got home from work, she came into my bedroom holding a box of feminine napkins in her hand. "I'll put these under the sink in the bathroom," she said very matter of factly, and then left the room to finish making dinner.

I was so bewildered. *Wait! Don't leave! I have so many questions. The teacher told me this only happens to girls and that it happens every month, but she didn't tell me anything else. Why does this happen to girls? Why does it hurt? Why does it happen every month? There's a lot of blood. Is that okay? Is that normal? Why didn't you tell me about this? I was really scared at school. I was so embarrassed. Did you know it happened in front of a bunch of kids at school? How do I go back to school after that? You really don't love me, do you?*

Brenda never talked with me about how my life had just changed and what was to come. No one did. My loyalty to Brenda as an ally against my "alcoholic" dad, waned. I felt alone and on my own, and I began to detach myself from everything and everyone, slowly fading away.

## Standing My Ground

Brandon had kept his end of the silent bargain for three years. We were still living in the first house. Brandon was seventeen, and I was eleven. I remember lying on Brandon's twin bed in the bedroom he shared with George. Brandon was sitting across from me on George's bed, and we were listening to his albums. It was a bright, sunny day and rays of light shone through the windows behind Brandon. Brandon suddenly stood up and left the room, and as he did, the light he had been blocking, pierced my eyes and I quickly closed them.

After a few minutes, I felt the piercing sunlight fade away and could sense Brandon was standing next to me. I opened my eyes and immediately saw Brandon holding his male genitalia in his hand and was thrusting it toward my mouth. It was strange, but somehow, I instinctively knew what Brandon wanted me to do. I lifted myself up and screeched in horror and began yelling, "No!" "No!" "No!" "No!"

Brandon knew immediately he had crossed the line and scurried out of the bedroom. This time I wasn't tolerating Brandon's behavior, and I wanted him to know I was crazy furious. I ran to my bedroom and slammed the door, hoping Brandon wouldn't try to come into my room.

*How could Brandon do that to me? What did he have in his hand? That was so gross! I can't believe he did that to me. I never thought he would do anything like this to me. I know he loves me, but why did he do that? Why do I still love him? God, please don't let Brandon do anything like that to me again.*

I never told Brenda or my dad about the things Brandon had done to me. I was too embarrassed to tell my dad, and I knew Brenda wouldn't believe me and might punish me for saying such bad things about her favorite son. But that day, I took a stand. I defended myself and changed the playing field of my relationship with Brandon. He never repeated the mistake, as I knew he wouldn't, and he did everything he could to apologize to me without speaking the words. For reasons I still don't understand, Brandon and I became closer because of the incident. I loved Brandon, and I wept uncontrollably when he died a year later.

## Brandon Dies

We were living in our second house when Brandon died. I remember walking down the hallway of a hospital and seeing Brenda sitting on a metal chair outside of one of the hospital rooms. As I approached, Brenda looked down the hall at me and began to scream at the top of her lungs, "He's gone Terry, He's gone!" I ran to Brenda and hugged her. I could feel the pain of loss writhing through her body. For the first time, I felt sad for Brenda.

I looked up and saw Brandon in the room, lying lifeless on a gurney. A tube was in his mouth and he was covered with blood. It was the first time I had seen death, apart from the times the birds flew into the picture window. I felt a wave of sadness overcome me and I began to weep. Brenda took me away from the room and told me it would be better to remember Brandon as he was and not as he is now. I was shocked by her sensitivity and the urge to protect me. It was foreign to me, but felt wonderful.

Brenda explained to me that Brandon was a passenger in his friend's car and was sitting behind the driver. Two other friends were also in the car; one sat beside the driver and the other sat in the back seat, next to Brandon. The driver moved into the opposing lane of traffic to pass a vehicle and didn't make it back into the right lane before hitting a vehicle head on. Brandon and the driver were killed instantly.

Brenda was checked-out for a long while after Brandon died and my life began a downward spiral. When Brandon died, I was left with parents who barely acknowledged my existence and a creepy step-brother. You'd think I would have been somewhat elated when Brandon died after the things he had done to me, but I was heartbroken. The only way to describe how I felt about Brandon when he died would be to say, I loved him as much as I hated him. I was closer to Brandon than I was to my dad or Brenda. Brandon was the only one in my family who had ever made me feel special and loved. Brandon was also the one who had humiliated me, betrayed me, and emotionally violated me. Love and hate; two strongly opposing forces, came to an agreement the day Brandon died. They agreed that love won out this time and they both wept.

## Waging War

When Brandon died, I was attending public school for the first time in my life. I remember what a shock it had been. There was no religious study, no church service on Wednesdays, and no paddle with holes drilled in it. The kids, even the girls, wore blue jeans and tennis shoes and the hallways in between classes rumbled with chaotic activity and loud conversation. It took me a bit, but I learned to navigate the hallways and juggle the many classrooms.

I was enthralled with the flapping of wings and my friends' display of individuality. I felt at home in the chaos and air of freedom and quickly began making friends. It was all very exciting to me. I was part of the group. I belonged. I fit in. Before long, I became one of them and didn't give two hoots that dad and Brenda would disapprove of my friends.

What I thought were sins, weren't even indiscretions to my new friends. Things like going over to a friend's house on the way home from school without first asking permission. The first time I did this, I was watching for the bolt of lightning to strike me. But after a few times of doing it, I felt liberated, powerful, and happy. When I was with my friends, I experienced intoxicating camaraderie, and I was hooked. It was like I had discovered a secret world to which I belonged.

It was almost unbearable living at home after Brandon died. I had lost my mother and now my brother; the only family that had ever loved me. Brenda became hollow and incessantly complained about my dad drinking. She became obsessed with George, which drove my dad even further into the background. I started lying to Brenda about where I was going and with whom. I didn't come home when I was supposed to and often toyed with the idea of never going home. I ran the streets at night with my friends, soaking in the freedom and my new-found independence. I began to wage war against dad and Brenda.

## First Love

We moved into the third house after only living in the second house for about a year, so the plan to run away from home had been placed on the back burner. I was relieved when I learned I was going to attend public school again. But, this time it would be different. Not only was I going to a new school, but I was going to be in the seventh grade. I was maturing physically and was now wearing a training bra and had more than a year of periods under my belt - No pun intended.

Within six months, I had a "boyfriend." David was an eighth-grader and had long dark hair, which I took as a sign of rebellion. I found I was attracted to and understood rebellion and a fight-the-system spirit. I was intrigued. We never formally declared ourselves boyfriend and girlfriend to each other, but we knew we were. We never kissed, but we would sometimes hold hands, as we walked with our friends to the Dairy Delight, after school.

One day while hanging out at the Dairy Delight, I saw David talking with another boy whom I hadn't seen before. He was very cute and I couldn't take my eyes off of him. I wondered if he had a girlfriend, and if he didn't, I wished I didn't have a boyfriend. I walked over to join in the conversation and David introduced me to Alex, who was in the eighth grade with David. I became nervous, almost giddy, and was afraid David would notice. David and I saw Alex frequently at the Dairy Delight and I soon learned that Alex had a girlfriend named Alice. At first, I was so jealous of Alice, having Alex as her boyfriend, but the more the four of us hung out together, the closer Alice and I became.

I continued to secretly pine over Alex, but thought there was no way a cute boy like him would ever want someone like me as his girlfriend. One wintry afternoon, David, Alice, Alex, and I were walking across a field on our way to Alice's house. David and Alice were walking about twenty feet ahead of Alex and I when Alex said, "If you were my girlfriend, I wouldn't walk so far ahead of you. I would walk with you."

I couldn't believe my ears! In my mind, I quickly replayed what Alex had said to see if I had heard him correctly. I had. *Quick! Say something! Let him know you like him and wish you were his girlfriend. You may not have another chance.*

"I wish you were my boyfriend instead of David," I said with a sheepish smile.

Alex looked to be happily surprised at what I said and smiled at me as if to say, "That can be arranged."

The following week, David and I walked to the Dairy Delight after school. As we walked in, I saw Alex and my heart leapt with excitement. I looked for Alice but didn't see her anywhere. David went over to talk with Alex while I got a soda. I was outside waiting for David when Alex walked up to me smiling. I could see David inside talking with some kids and wondered what was going on.

"I broke up with Alice," Alex announced.

I couldn't believe what I was hearing.

Before I could say anything, Alex said, " I talked with David and told him I broke up with Alice because I like you and want you to be my girlfriend."

"What did David say?" I asked.

"He said he's okay with it," Alex replied.

I looked inside the Dairy Delight. David was still inside, talking and laughing with his friends. *Is this really happening? I can't believe Alex told David he likes me and wants me to be his girlfriend! I'm so excited! I'm so happy!* I looked back at Alex smiling, as if to say, "Of course I'll be your girlfriend!"

Alex lived only a few blocks from my house, so everyday we would walk home from school together, sometimes with Alex's sister, Adrienne. Adrienne was in the same grade as I was and we soon became best friends, which worked out well, as I could tell Brenda I was hanging out with Adrienne when I wanted to see Alex.

Alex and I were first loves and spent every moment we could together. Alex would come to my house late at night and throw pebbles at my bedroom window, hoping I would hear them and sneak outside to see him, if only for a few minutes. We wrote each other love letters, professing our love for one another; letters I would hide away in an unsuspecting place in my bedroom. I thought about him day and night and couldn't wait until the time I could see him again. We immersed ourselves in each other's love and adoration, and one moonlit night, we lovingly gave our virginity to each other.

## Reflection of Hope

The emotional neglect I experienced as a child left me love-starved, both emotionally and physically. Not a day went by that I didn't crave a loving touch or long to hear the words "I love you," but day after day, I came up empty. It wasn't just the need to feel loved that I craved, I had a deep desire to know what it felt like to love someone.

I talk about wanting love and wanting to love, but the funny thing is, when you grow up without it, you don't even know it is love you're looking for. Until I met Alex, the only time I had heard the word love was in church or in a bible study class. There I had heard about God's love for us and that God is Love, but I didn't really know what love was. I had no reference.

When Alex came into my life, I knew I was loved, and I wanted to give love in return. What I had been searching for all those years was overflowing in my heart, and I finally had a name for it; Love. It was a powerful force that swept me away and became my reason for being.

In the scriptures, we find four unique types of love. Eros is romantic love, storge is familial love, philia is brotherly love, and agape is God's love for us[1]. As I have walked through this journey of life, I've learned that eros, storge, and philia are all fallible because they are human love. The only infallible love is agape or God's love. We as humans, cannot possibly fathom a love like the love God has for us. Human love is conditional. We say, "I love you unconditionally," but do we? Our love for our other half or our "brother" or our family is all based on conditions we set in our mind. The minute those conditions are no longer met by one of us, the deal is off. I'm not saying that all humans are lying when they say they love someone. I'm sure they do. What I am saying is human love is like humans: it's imperfect, flawed, and frail.

Unlike human love, God's love for us is perfect and true. God doesn't say the deal is off when we sin. On the contrary.

God sent his Son to die on the cross to pay the price for our sins so that we could be with him in the Kingdom of Heaven forever. The Apostle John explained God's love for us by saying, "This is how God showed his love among us: He sent his one and only Son into the world that we might live through him. This is love: not that we loved God, but that he loved us and sent his Son as an atoning sacrifice for our sins," (1 John 4:9-10 NIV). Wow! Did you catch the part about "This is love: not that we loved God, but that he loved us and sent his Son as an atoning sacrifice for our sins?" Unlike human love, God's love is unconditional. Unlike human love, God never stops loving us, no matter what.

My life has been filled with love from family, friends, and significant others, but it will never compare to the love God has for me or the love I have for God. The Apostle John tells us "God is love, and the one who abides in love abides in God, and God abides in him," (1 John 4:16 NASB 1995). I pray for the day when we all let God abide in us.

## Scriptures of Hope

✝ For I am convinced [and continue to be convinced—beyond any doubt] that neither death, nor life, nor angels, nor principalities, nor things present and threatening, nor things to come, nor powers, nor height, nor depth, nor any other created thing, will be able to separate us from the [unlimited] love of God, which is in Christ Jesus our Lord. (Romans 8:38-39 AMP)

✝ See how very much our Father loves us, for he calls us his children, and that is what we are! But the people who belong to this world don't recognize that we are God's children because they don't know him. (1 John 3:1 NLT)

✝ But you, Lord, are a compassionate and gracious God, slow to anger, abounding in love and faithfulness. (Psalm 86:15 NIV)

✝ No one has ever seen God. But if we love each other, God lives in us, and his love is brought to full expression in us. (1 John 4:12 NLT)

✝ Dear friends, let us love one another, for love comes from God. Everyone who loves has been born of God and knows God. (1 John 4:7 NIV)

✝ For I know the thoughts that I think toward you, says the Lord, thoughts of peace and not of evil, to give you a future and a hope. (Jeremiah 29:11 NKJV)

✝ For I hold you by your right hand— I, the Lord your God. And I say to you, Don't be afraid. I am here to help you. (Isaiah 41:13 NLT)

✝ Love is patient and kind; love does not envy or boast; it is not arrogant or rude. It does not insist on its own way; it is not irritable or resentful; it does not rejoice at wrongdoing, but rejoices with the truth. Love bears all things, believes all things, hopes all things, endures all things. (1 Corinthians 13:4-7 ESV)

☦ So do not fear, for I am with you; do not be dismayed, for I am your God. I will strengthen you and help you; I will uphold you with my righteous right hand. (Isaiah 41:10 NIV)

☦ But the fruit of the Spirit [the result of His presence within us] is love [unselfish concern for others], joy, [inner] peace, patience [not the ability to wait, but how we act while waiting], kindness, goodness, faithfulness, gentleness, self-control. Against such things there is no law. (Galatians 5:22-23 AMP)

# Chapter 3

## *I Died With You*

*Jesus said, "Let the little children come to me, and do not hinder them, for the kingdom of heaven belongs to such as these."*

— Matthew 19:14 NIV

"Are you pregnant?" Brenda asked. "I haven't seen any pads in the garbage for two months."

It was Saturday, mid-morning, house cleaning day. I thought about the question. I knew what being pregnant was, but I didn't understand why she was asking me that question.

"I don't know," I replied, shrugging my shoulders.

"Is Alex the father?" Brenda asked.

It wasn't until Brenda asked this question that I realized why I might be pregnant.

"Uh-huh," I replied.

Brenda got this look on her face that was part disgust and

part fear, which frightened me. Brenda didn't say anything more; she just walked away.

When I told Alex I might be pregnant, his face took on a look of sheer terror. Alex's father was in the military and was very strict.

"Are you sure?" Alex asked.

"I'm not sure. I didn't even know I could be pregnant until Brenda asked me if I was," I said, as I began to cry.

Alex began to pace. The look of terror had not left his face.

"If my parents find out, I'm dead," Alex exclaimed.

When Alex said this, I knew he didn't want me to have the baby. I couldn't blame him, really. He probably would be in a lot of trouble, mainly because I was thirteen and he was fourteen, which was and is way too young to have a baby.

"Brenda wants you to come to our house to talk about what we're going to do." Alex shook his head, agreeing to the meeting.

The following Saturday, Alex came to the house as planned. Alex, Brenda, and I sat in the corner of the living room where the chairs were arranged in a triangle. I sat in a chair in the corner, with Alex on my right and Brenda on my left. I sensed no one else was in the house. It was just the three of us.

"What do you want to do?" Brenda asked.

"I want to have the baby," I replied, looking at Alex to see his response to my declaration.

It was as I expected; Alex looked petrified and said nothing. The last thing he wanted was for me to have the baby and have there be a chance his parents would find out it was his.

"You can't keep it," Brenda snapped. I wanted to keep it, but now I realized it wasn't a possibility, as Brenda didn't seem willing to let me raise my baby in her house.

"Well, I guess I could give it up for adoption," I said, looking at Alex, urging him for a response. Alex sat in the chair in terrified silence. I looked at Brenda to see her reaction to my suggestion, and what I saw was frightening.

"You can't have this baby," Brenda commanded.

"What do you mean?" I asked.

"You are going to have an abortion," Brenda said coldly.

My heart began pounding, and I felt like I couldn't breathe. *No. She didn't just say I had to have an abortion, did she? She did. No, I won't have an abortion. I won't kill my baby. It's wrong to kill a baby! You know that Brenda. How can you tell me to have an abortion when you know it's a sin and it's murdering a baby? I hate you!*

I looked at Alex, waiting for him to protest, but his objection never came. Instead, he looked at Brenda and said, "I have some money I can give you for the abortion." *Oh my God! You brought money for an abortion? How could you do that? I thought you loved me. Don't you love our baby? Don't you want our baby? How can you want to kill our baby? I don't believe this is happening.*

Alex stood up, handed Brenda some money, and left. I had never felt so alone and unloved in my life. I had been taught in school and church that having an abortion was wrong. How could Brenda go to church every Sunday and pretend she was a good Christian and then tell me to have an abortion? The thought of it sickened me. I hated Brenda. I didn't want to kill my baby. I looked at Brenda with extreme hatred and went to my room to cry.

## Please Forgive Me

My dad and I drove an hour and thirty minutes to the clinic in silence. I remember wondering why it was so far away from our house. I later realized the distance helped to keep the reason for the trip covert. The entrance of the clinic opened into a large room with painted concrete floors and alternating rows of black plastic chairs and benches where people could sit and wait. I sat down while dad walked up to the window on the other side of the room to tell them we were there. The lady at the desk behind the window handed my dad a clipboard with papers held tightly by a clip fastened to the top. My dad took the clipboard, sat down beside me and proceeded to fill out the forms with a pen that was tied to the clip with a string.

As I looked around the room, I noticed the few women that were waiting were all much older than I was. Some looked uneasy and some looked like they were waiting for a bus, but they all took turns staring at me. I began to feel uncomfortable and wished my dad would hurry and finish filling out the forms. After a few minutes, my dad got up and took the clipboard to the lady behind the window. They exchanged a few words and then my dad returned and took his place next to me. The door to the right of the window swung open. A nurse appeared and called out my name. My dad got up and I followed him through the door. We walked into a room with a desk and two chairs in front of it, and each of us sat in one of the chairs. A doctor came in, sat behind the desk, and started talking with my dad. I didn't understand what the doctor was saying and my dad just kept shaking his head up and down and saying, "uh huh" as the doctor spoke.

When the doctor and my dad were done talking, a nurse came into the room and led me to the room next door. In the room there was a padded table with paper covering it and two metal bars protruding from the bottom. Each metal bar had what looked like a horse stirrup attached to the end, and I wondered what they were. In a monotone voice, the nurse instructed me to take off my clothes from the waist down and put on the gown that was lying on the table. As she left the room, she told me a doctor would be there in a few minutes.

I could hear people shuffling outside the door as I took off my pants and underwear. I was hurrying, trying to get the gown on before anyone walked into the room. I stepped up on the table and sat on the paper covering, tucking the gown under my legs and buttocks so my backside wasn't exposed. After a few minutes, the same doctor that spoke with my dad walked into the room and closed the door behind him. With a blank expression on his face, the doctor explained what would happen next. He said he was going to insert a seaweed rod into my cervix that would stay there overnight, so I would be dilated for the procedure the next day.

With the same blank expression, the doctor instructed me to lie back, scoot my butt to the end of the table, and put my feet in the stirrups. I was shocked at his directions, but with great hesitation, I carried out his instructions. Extreme tension took over my body as I lie there, clutching the sides of the table. The doctor told me to relax as he inserted a cold, metal object into my vagina.

"You may feel some cramping now," he said, inserting the seaweed rod into my cervix.

I could feel my body tense up even more, and I prayed this would be over soon.

I walked into the waiting area and saw my dad sitting in one of the black plastic chairs. He was sitting very stoically, purposefully avoiding eye contact with anyone in the room. When he saw me enter the room, his face dropped, and he smiled at me sadly. As we left the clinic, he gently placed his hand on my back as a gesture of sympathy. I couldn't remember the last time my dad touched me, not counting the time he beat my bare bottom with his belt. It felt nice, but did nothing to mitigate his complicity. I hated my dad for allowing this to happen.

*Why hadn't he stood up for me against Brenda? How could he go along with this?*

On the drive home, the silence was thick and I hoped my dad wouldn't see me crying. The next day, as we drove to the clinic, my dad futilely attempted to lighten the mood with small talk. I was numb.

*I don't want to do this! I don't want to kill my baby! I can't believe this is really happening. Is it too late? Did the seaweed kill my baby? Maybe it didn't. Maybe my baby is still alive and they could take the seaweed out and I can still have my baby.*

The nurse escorted me to the same room I was in the day before and repeated the drill about taking my clothes off below the waist and putting on the gown.

"You can put your clothes over there," she said, pointing to a chair as she left the room.

I couldn't help but notice a large metal machine sitting on a cart next to the paper-covered table. The machine looked like a vacuum cleaner canister that had long hoses connected to it. I put on the gown and sat down on the table, staring at the machine and wondered why it was there and what it was.

A few minutes later, the doctor and two nurses entered the room and began preparing for the procedure. The doctor sat down on a stool at the end of the table and told me to lie back, scoot my butt to the end of the table, and put my feet in the stirrups. A nurse pushed a metal tray of instruments next to the doctor as he positioned the machine closer to him on the other side. A nurse inserted a needle into my right arm, securing it with white tape, and then took her position next to me.

The doctor began his work without uttering a word. I had no idea what was going to happen or what he was doing to me. I began to feel cramping and grabbed the hand of the nurse standing beside me.

She gently squeezed my hand as if to say, "I'm here with you."

The machine became louder and I looked over to see what was going on. It was then that I saw the end of one of the clear hoses connected to the machine was between my legs and had been inserted into my vagina. The machine began to whir, and I saw blood and pieces of my baby being sucked up through the hose and into the machine.

*Oh my God! That's my baby being sucked up through that tube. I swear I saw a little leg. Maybe it was an arm. Oh my God. I can't bear this. I'm sorry baby. I didn't want to do this. I'm so sorry. Please forgive me.*

I turned away horrified and the nurse squeezed my hand.

## Lost Faith

I could hear Brenda open my bedroom door to see what I was doing and why I wasn't leaving with them to go to church. I was in bed under the covers, pretending to be asleep. Without saying a word, Brenda carefully closed the door and announced that I wasn't going to church today. After a few Sundays, Brenda stopped opening my bedroom door. To me, Brenda and my dad were religious hypocrites who had completely destroyed my faith in God. I was so angry with God for letting my baby die that I never wanted to set foot in a church again.

Neither Brenda nor my dad ever talked with me about the abortion. They never told me they were sorry for making me kill my baby. They never sat down with me and asked me how I was doing or cared enough to try to figure out how we got there, to begin with. They never talked with me about love, relationships, sex, birth control, or what life would look like from now on. They never told me they loved me or that God loved me, despite my sexual indiscretion. There were no loving words, no comforting embraces, no tears. Just the familiar silence.

I rarely spoke to my dad and only spoke to Brenda to tell her where I was going and when I would be home. I hated both of them and couldn't stand living in the same house with them. When I was home, I was in my bedroom and only came out to shower and eat. Brenda no longer invited me to go shopping with her or go to the grocery store. My dad faded even further into the background, but this time, I didn't care; I preferred it. I began to separate myself from them and spent as much time as I could away from home. I started coming home late from school and would brush Brenda off when she'd ask me where I had been. Brenda soon got the message that I didn't care much about anything, least of all her or her rules.

The days went by, and Alex and I tried to pretend the abortion never happened. Alex never wanted to talk about the abortion. I could tell he felt as if he had dodged a huge bullet and just wanted to go on as if it never happened. Alex never showed any grief over the loss of our baby. He never said he was sorry for turning his back on me and our baby. I would never forgive him for that, and felt myself separating from Alex as well.

The next school year, I started hanging out with some kids who were part of the renegade group who would sneak off to the smoking spot away from the school. Standing in a circle with the rest of the kids, smoking a Kool menthol cigarette, I felt free of the pain and oppression of life. My new friends made me feel empowered to forge my way and find my own happiness. They understood betrayal and loneliness and took me in as one of their own.

I began cutting classes with them, and sometimes we would hang out with some of their high school friends. On our way back to school one day, my friend stopped and held out his hand. In it were some white tablets.

"What are those?" I asked.

"It's speed," he replied. "Do you want to do some?"

I was hesitant, but curious.

"What does it feel like?" I asked.

"It speeds you up and makes you high. You'll like it," he said with a gleam in his eye.

"I don't know. I've never done anything like that before," I told him.

My friend could sense my reluctance and said, "Here. Take a half. You'll be okay. I'll do some too."

He broke one of the tablets in half, handed it to me, and then picked up a whole one. He looked at me as if to say, "Here we go," and then put the tablet in his mouth. I followed suit. At first, I was afraid to take it, but as the speed took effect, I began to enjoy the high. Needless to say, my friend and I didn't go back to school that day.

Finally, school let out for the summer, and I could spend my days with Alex and my friends. Although Alex and I spent less time together, we were still trying to keep the relationship together. Before I had the abortion, I saw Alex and I getting married and spending the rest of our lives together, but things had changed, and I no longer had that vision. I knew in my heart we could never go back to the way things were before the baby. Too much damage had been done. I think we both knew this, but it was much too hard for us to let go.

## Reflection of Hope

Even at thirteen years old, I knew having an abortion was wrong. Our family went to church every Sunday. Brenda was a bookkeeper for the Lutheran Church. I went to a parochial school until I was eleven years old. How do parents who raise their child in a religious environment make a decision that their daughter will have an abortion and we will see that it happens? Why couldn't I have the child and give it up for adoption? Why did I have to kill the baby?

I will never understand. Until then I had been a good girl, but the day I had the abortion, I became a murderer committing the ultimate sin and Brenda and my dad were my accomplices.

Abortion is an extremely violent act. The British Pregnancy Advisory Service explains that a vacuum aspiration, aka vacuum abortion, "...uses gentle suction to remove the pregnancy[1]..." What the British Pregnancy Advisory Service doesn't explain is exactly what "remove the pregnancy" really entails. In the 1984 film, *The Silent Scream*, viewers are shown a 12-week old baby being killed via a suction abortion. The film's narrator, Dr. Bernard Nathanson (1926 – 2011), was a former abortionist who was responsible for some 60,000 abortions before becoming pro-life. In the film, Dr. Nathanson describes how the suction tip of the machine will begin to tear the child apart. The pieces of the baby are torn away, one by one, until all that remains are shards of body and the head itself. The head will be too large to go through the suction tube, so forceps are used to grasp the free-floating head of the child, at which time, the head is crushed and the contents of the head are removed, as well as the bones of the head[2].

After Dr. Nathanson's detailed description of the abortion procedure, an actual abortion of a 12-week-old fetus, as seen through ultrasound, is shown. Viewers can see that when the suction tip begins to enter the uterus, the baby violently moves away from it, trying to escape and the baby's heart rate increases to 200 bpm. At one point during the process, the ultrasound video is paused, and Dr. Nathanson points out how the mouth of the baby is open as if it is screaming, and he refers to it as "the silent scream[3]."

The million-dollar question is, when does life begin? Some say life begins when the fetus is viable, which means the baby can survive outside of the womb. Some say life begins at conception. That's certainly what I believed and still do to this day. In his presentation called *Abortion,* on RightNow Media, Theologian R.C. Sproul talks about the natural law viewpoint of when life begins and states that a person's genetic code is fully established at conception. The baby's heart begins to beat between eighteen and twenty-five weeks. At eight weeks, brain waves can be detected, and the baby has fingerprints. Between twelve and thirteen weeks, the baby sucks its thumb and recoils from pain.

Having an abortion is hands down the deepest regret of my life and a memory that time will never diminish. To this day, I remember every detail of it. The horror of it. The profound sadness. I couldn't forgive myself for killing my child, nor Brenda and my dad for leaving me no choice. I couldn't forgive Alex for not wanting our child and being so willing to destroy it. I blamed myself for not rising up and vehemently refusing to have an abortion. I blamed myself for going through with it. I cursed God and blamed him for allowing it to happen. I dismissed God and became a lost soul.

Having an abortion turned my life upside down. I lost my belief in God and began to flounder through life. It sent me on a desperate and diligent search to be loved and to fill the gaping hole in my heart. I felt alone, like I had been cast aside, and wanted nothing more than to run until my legs would no longer carry me. Profound grief engulfed me, and I envisioned death as my only relief.

It would take fifty-one years for me to forgive Brenda, my

dad, Alex, and myself. Fifty-one years to realize I was not to blame for the death of my child and I wasn't a murderer. And fifty-one years to come home to God, where I found peace. Trying to make sense of the terrible things that happen in our lives can test our faith. We ask, "Why did God take my child? Why did God let my marriage fail? Why did God allow the company to lay me off?" We blame God and consider these things as punishment.

Adam and Eve gave Satan the lease on earth. Satan wants to be God. He wants to be worshiped by us. He wants us to be on his side. But Satan doesn't have the ability to love, and he can't save us or grant us mercy or grace, and he certainly can't love us. God wants us in His family and gives us a choice of life with Him or death by following Satan. God gives us free agency because He only wants us as part of His family if we want to be a part of it. God isn't going to make us love Him or make us be part of His family, although he wants nothing more.

Sometimes bad things happen in our lives because it is a result of a decision we made. Sometimes bad things happen because it is Satan's effort to guide us away from God and get us on his side. Sometimes bad things happen because they are part of the plan to empower us to serve others or strengthen us. Whatever the reason, God is always there to comfort us and will not allow Satan to craft the weight of life as something more than we can endure. God will never forsake us and is standing by, waiting for our prayers and our cries for help. Ask God for help and for His protection. Ask Him to guide you and give you understanding. Ask Him for peace.

Looking back on my life, I can see the abortion and all

the pain in my life was somehow part of God's plan, as were all the hardships to come. It was a painful stepping stone that changed life's compass and sent me on a path I would not have taken otherwise. It wasn't until I came home that I was able to surrender and give all of life's trials to Him. It wasn't until I came home that I was able to find peace and to forgive.

## Scriptures of Hope

✝ If I walk in the thick of danger, You will preserve my life from the anger of my enemies. You will extend Your hand; Your right hand will save me. (Psalm 138:7 CSB)

✝ Peace I leave with you; my peace I give to you. Not as the world gives do I give to you. Let not your hearts be troubled, neither let them be afraid. (John 14:27 ESV)

✝ Don't be afraid, for I am with you. Don't be discouraged, for I am your God. I will strengthen you and help you. I will hold you up with my victorious right hand. (Isaiah 41:10 NLT)

✝ He healeth the broken in heart, and bindeth up their wounds. (Psalms 147:3 KJV)

✝ Give all your worries and cares to God, for he cares about you. (1 Peter 5:7 NLT)

✝ God is our shelter and strength, always ready to help in times of trouble. (Psalms 46:1 GNT)

✝ The righteous cry, and the LORD heareth, and delivereth them out of all their troubles. (Psalm 34:17 KJV)

✝ This means that anyone who belongs to Christ has become a new person. The old life is gone; a new life has begun! (2 Corinthians 5:17 NLT)

✝ And I will forgive their wickedness, and I will never again remember their sins. (Hebrews 8:12 NLT)

✝ Trust in the Lord with all your heart. Never rely on what you think you know. Remember the Lord in everything you do, and he will show you the right way. (Proverbs 3:5-6 GNT)

# Chapter 4

## *Runaway*

*"And where are you going?"*

*"I dunno," said the Spangled Boy. "I'm running from, not to."*

— E. Nesbit, Wet Magic

My anger and disdain toward Brenda and my dad continued to fester, and it got to the point where I could hardly bear to live in the same house with them. Not caring what either of them thought or wanted, I would spend days away at a friend's house without telling them where I was or when I would be home. When I would come home, neither Brenda nor my dad would ask me where I had been or what I had been doing and there were no attempts to punish me for my misconduct. Going home became harder and harder until, one day, I walked out the front door with no intention of returning.

For the first few days, I walked the streets, hung out with

friends, and slept in fields at night. A friend of a friend found out I was sleeping in fields and told me I could sleep at her house for a while, but I would have to go in the house after her mom went to work that night. My friend and her mom lived in a small white house a few blocks from the bar where my friend's mom worked. Her mom was a bartender, and she would leave for work at about five o'clock in the evening. When it became dusk, we took up a sentry position outside the house and waited until my friend's mom left for work. When the coast was clear, we went inside and settled in for the night.

At first, when her mom would wake up the next day and see me there, she would just think I was there hanging out with her daughter. After all, it was summer, and we were out of school. But after seeing me there every day for about two weeks, my friend's mom began to ask questions about why I was always there. When my friend told her I had run away from home, her mom told her I had to leave. I had nowhere to go and didn't want to live on the streets, so reluctantly, I went home.

When I walked through the door, there wasn't a prodigal-son welcome for me or gestures of relief that I was alive and safe. Brenda and my dad continued on with life, never missing a beat. I'm certain if the family dog had been lost for days and had returned home, she would have received a warmer welcome home than I had. I had always felt unloved; now, I felt unwelcome.

It wasn't long before I ran away from home again, but this time it was short-lived, as my friend's sister called the police and I was arrested for being a runaway. My friend and I were at her sister's apartment just hanging out, when my friend's sister came into the bedroom and told me someone was at the door for me. I was confused, as no one knew I was there. I went to see who was at the door and saw two police officers standing in the living room. My heart sank. I was busted. One of the officers asked me my name, and when I told him, he said I had been reported as a runaway and they were taking me to the juvenile detention center. I felt embarrassed and avoided making eye contact with anyone in the room as the officer searched me, put handcuffs on me, and led me out of the apartment.

My heart was pounding as the officers escorted me to the police car. I could see people in the apartment complex looking at me with their judgmental eyes and wanting to scream at them, "I'M NOT A CRIMINAL!" My fear intensified as the officer opened the back of his patrol car and told me to get in. The handcuffs dug into my back and my contorted hands as I sat back against the seat while the officer fastened my seat belt. I watched the officer through the divider as he got into the car and began speaking on the police radio, telling the dispatcher he was transporting me to the juvenile detention center.

*Oh my God! I'm handcuffed and sitting in the back seat of a police car. I'm really afraid. What's going to happen to me? Is the juvenile detention center like a jail for kids? Are they going to put me in a jail cell? Will I have a cellmate? Will I get beat up? Am I a criminal? Can you just take me home? I won't run away again, I promise. I didn't know you could go to jail for running away from home. How long will I be there? I'm really afraid.*

The police officer parked his police car and told the dispatcher he had arrived at the juvenile detention center.

The officer helped me get out of the police car and escorted me into the building. We walked through two sets of security doors before we entered the check-in area. I sat on a bench and waited for the officer while he filled out some paperwork and checked me into the facility. When he was done, he walked over to me and took off the handcuffs, and then handed me off to a detention center worker.

The female worker was holding a security door open and motioned to me to go through the door and into an area where she searched me. She confiscated my personal belongings, putting them in a plastic bag with a label with my name on it, and then put me in a large holding room with about thirty male and female juvenile delinquents. The heavy security door slammed shut behind me, and I felt a rush of fear surge through my body. I stood on the painted concrete floor and took stock of my surroundings.

Solid painted concrete walls were behind and on both sides of me, with a painted concrete bench protruding from each of them. In front of me was a painted concrete wall with a large window and a doorway to the right. Looking through the window, I saw more kids in another painted concrete room about half as big as the one I was in. The rooms were bare. There were no beds, tables, or chairs-no blankets, pillows, magazines, or television - nothing. Security cameras were mounted on the ceiling in all four corners of the room, and the workers regularly came in and walked around the room checking on all of the kids.

The boys and girls were scattered around the room, some on the concrete benches and some on the floor. Most of them were older kids, but a few were younger than I was. Most of them kept to themselves and made it clear they weren't interested in engaging in any conversation. Some looked like they were high on drugs, and some smelled like alcohol. They all looked lost.

I saw a vacant spot on the floor next to a concrete bench and walked toward it, hoping the kids nearby wouldn't object to me squatting there. I sat down on the cold concrete floor with my back against the concrete bench and waited for those around me to react. With no objections raised, I claimed the few square feet as my own and began to wait; for what, I wasn't sure, but I waited. It was getting late, and I was exhausted. I realized I had fallen asleep when I was awoken abruptly by one of the workers.

"Wake up," she said as she kicked my feet.

I quickly sat up and looked at her as if to say, "Sorry. It won't happen again."

As I watched the worker walk away, I thought, "Why don't they want me to sleep? It must be part of my punishment." I was so tired and was fighting to stay awake. I spent the next hour or so repeatedly catching myself dropping my head to sleep and forcing myself to snap out of it and stay awake. It must have been in the middle of the night when one of the workers walked up to me and told me they were moving me to the smaller room. I wondered why, but didn't ask and did what I was told.

As I walked through the door into the smaller room, I noticed a solid wall on my right and in front of me, but the wall to my left also had a large window. You couldn't see through the window; it was dark on the other side and very bright in the smaller room. There weren't nearly as many kids in the smaller room as there were in the large room, and again, I wondered why they moved me to the smaller room and what differentiated the kids in the smaller from those in the large room. I was so tired I didn't have the energy to think about it, so I took a seat on the floor and waited. I noticed that even though cameras were mounted to the ceiling, the workers' rounds didn't include the smaller room. I decided to test the waters and go to sleep.

When I woke up, I realized I had been sleeping for quite a while without receiving a demand from a worker to stay awake. The space on the other side of the window was now visible, and I could see a room with a long counter and a waiting area. I watched as people entered the room and approached the person behind the counter. After conversing briefly with whoever was behind the counter, the person would sit in the waiting area. I continued to watch for a few minutes when I recognized a man who walked in and spoke with the person behind the counter. *Oh my God! That's my dad! He must be here to take me home. I'm so relieved and so excited to be getting out of here, even if it means I have to go home.*

A few minutes later, a worker came into the smaller room and told me my dad was there to take me home. I followed him to the room on the other side of the window where I saw my dad sitting on a chair in the waiting room. I walked up to him and he stood up and walked out the door without saying a word. I followed him to his car and got in. We drove in silence. I thought we were going home, but my dad took a different route and drove through the neighborhood where my friend and her bartender mom lived. I thought this was odd, but then I thought maybe my dad was going to stop at one of the nearby stores on the way home.

"Where do you want to be dropped off?" my dad asked.

I was confused and couldn't believe what I was hearing. *Wow! He's really going to drop me off wherever I want him to. I can't believe this. He really doesn't want me to come home. I must be such a disappointment to him. I can't believe my dad is going to drop me off on the street and doesn't care what happens to me. If you don't want me, I'll go.* I pointed to a corner close to my friend's house, and my dad pulled the car over and stopped. Without saying a word, I exited the car and shut the door. I watched for my dad to look at me to at least convey a silent goodbye, but he never did; he just drove away and didn't look back.

I went to my friend's house who lived nearby, told her and her mom what had just happened, and asked if I could stay with them for a while. My friend's mom must have felt sorry for me because she agreed to let me stay there for a few weeks. We still had a good part of the summer left before we had to return to school, so we spent our days hanging out with friends or at the shopping center a few blocks from my friend's house. Sometimes, I would see Alex, and we would go to the arcade or the bowling alley. We still loved each other and were trying to regain some degree of normalcy, but I could feel myself slipping away.

My friend and I got a job selling flowers on the street corner. It didn't pay much, but I was paid cash after every shift. One day when I was working, one of my flower customers invited me to a party he was having later that night. He was probably about nineteen years old and very cute. When I got off work, I told my friend about the party I was invited to and we decided to go. The party was at an apartment where my flower customer and his friend lived.

The apartment was packed with people; none of whom either of us knew. It took a bit, but I finally found my flower customer playing pool in the living room. *It looks so weird to have just a pool table and some chairs in a living room. I wish I had my own apartment where I could party with my friends all night.*

There was what seemed like an endless supply of beer and alcohol at the party and there was no shortage of pot being passed around. I'm sure there were other drugs there, as some of the partiers looked high as a kite on something that definitely wasn't pot. My friend and I partied with my flower customer and his roommate late into the night. I woke up the next day on the floor next to the pool table with my flower customer lying next to me. I had an "I wish I were dead" hangover, and my throat was raw from smoking pot and cigarettes all night. I got up slowly using the pool table to steady myself, and then carefully navigated to the bathroom. The bathroom and the toilet bowl looked all too familiar as I saw flashbacks of me hugging the throne and vomiting in my hair. As I came out of the bathroom, I began looking for my friend. I looked in every room in the apartment and she was nowhere to be found. I used the telephone in the kitchen to call her, but no one answered the phone.

*Now what do I do? How could my friend leave me here alone? I hope she's okay. Damn I feel like sh–. How do I get back to my friend's house? I don't even know where I am. I have no money. Maybe my flower customer will take me to my friend's house. I don't want to wake him up. I'll just sit and wait for him to wake up and then I'll ask him for a ride to my friend's house.*

I let my flower customer wake up, go to the bathroom,

and smoke a cigarette before I asked him if he could give me a ride to my friend's house. He said he would when his roommate came home with the car later that night. I called my friend later that afternoon and she answered the phone. When I asked if her mom could come and get me, she said she was in trouble for not coming home last night, and her mom wouldn't let me stay there anymore. *Oh great. Now what do I do? Where am I going to sleep? How am I going to get to work?*

When I told my flower customer I could no longer stay at my friend's house, he said I could stay with him for a few days. I was grateful for the offer and gladly accepted it, but after the second night, I woke up knowing I had no choice but to go home. The thing was, I didn't know if Brenda and my dad would let me come home, but I had to try. I called Brenda and asked her if she would pick me up. She said she would, and I gave her the address. I waited outside for Brenda and was actually glad to see her little baby blue Ford Falcon pull into the parking lot of the apartment complex. The Falcon had been Brandon's car. When Brandon died, Brenda couldn't bear to let it go and drove it to feel closer to him. We drove home in silence. That was the last time I ran away from home.

When the summer was over, I started my first year of high school. My days of cutting classes were over, and I tried to buckle down and fly straight. Later in the school year, there was an opportunity to go to a college campus and meet a group of attorneys who would speak about what it was like to be an attorney and what it would take to become one. I was fascinated with the law, and for the first time in my life, I became excited about my future. The event was more than I expected, and I was completely enthralled with the attorneys and their presentations. I went home afterward, knowing that becoming an attorney was what I wanted to do with my life.

I was so excited as I told Brenda about the event and told her I wanted to become an attorney. I really didn't expect much of a reaction from Brenda, but I certainly didn't expect it when she said, "I don't think you could do that because you don't like to read." My dream was crushed with a single remark as I heard, "You won't make it through law school because you're not smart enough." Brenda's unsupporting remark changed the course of my life. I no longer felt like I could dare to dream or thought I was capable of reaching a goal like becoming an attorney. My future looked bleak, and I lost all interest in school.

I was so tired of being knocked down and getting back up only to be knocked down again. My self-esteem was in the toilet, and I didn't like myself very much. That same school year, Alex and I began to fade away, and by the end of the summer, we went our separate ways. The breakup was painful. I still loved Alex and would carry a torch for him for the next 51 years. I became a loner, feeling lost, pathetic, and as if I had imploded. I had no friends, no Alex, no home, no dreams, no aspirations. Only emptiness and regret.

## Reflection of Hope

Oftentimes, running away from a problem does nothing to solve the problem; it only creates more problems. We will never escape from having trials in our lives. They are part of the fabric of life. They are inevitable and every bit as necessary as the good times. Yes, I said our trials are necessary. Sometimes, the only way to learn a lesson is through strife. These lessons are valuable and can make us wise if we let them. You see, without them, we would never learn, never grow and evolve, and never appreciate the good in life. Life is full of contrasts that guide us. How can we know daylight without knowing darkness, satiety without hunger, or peace without conflict? We should embrace our trials and allow them to guide us, to teach us, and to mold us.

We go through life making plans and create a roadmap that will lead us to our sought-after destinations. We feel so in control of our destiny and have such high expectations that everything will turn out just as we planned. The fact is, we don't have full control over our destiny; we only have the gift of choice. We can choose our outlook, our attitude, and our reactions. And what we should choose will not always be easy and will most likely feel very counterintuitive. This is when we must react with our "wise" mind instead of our "emotional" mind, and running away is usually not the right choice unless you are running from a flock of predatory birds or Megatron.

Brenda's remark about my wanting to go to law school made me feel I wasn't smart enough for such a lofty goal. My reaction and choice was to believe her and lose interest in school altogether, which sent me on a very different path. The next school year, I got married and dropped out of high school. The choice to drop out of high school made life a lot more difficult for me than it would have been had I graduated and gone to college. But looking back, I can see how the trials that decision created gave me the desire to make something of myself and to make a better life. I definitely didn't take the easy road, but I learned valuable lessons about life that I wouldn't have learned otherwise. I learned how valuable an education can be and the doors it can open. I learned self-discipline and that hard work pays off in the end. But most importantly, I realized I was smart, and I could be successful, and that Brenda was wrong about me.

Looking back, I don't know or understand the reasons for all of my trials, and I probably never will. But that's okay. I do know that all of my trials have given me wisdom and the ability to know a greater depth of joy. I also know that since God has welcomed me home, I have tremendous peace. We spend our lives worrying, being anxious, and ruminating over problems when we should give our worries and troubles over to God. Before I came home, I worried about everything. My anxiety was through the roof, and instead of sleeping, I spent my nights obsessing over my troubles. But, when I surrendered to God and began living my life for Him, I was able to give my troubles to Him, knowing He would take care of me because He loves me so very much. I don't worry anymore. I give my worries and wishes to the Lord and let Him handle them. I know He will provide me with what I need and will watch over me, as I have seen it happen many times in my life. Now, instead of worrying, I thank the Lord for carrying the weight for me.

## Scriptures of Hope

✝ Anxiety in a man's heart weighs him down, but a good word makes him glad. (Proverbs 12:25 ESV)

† Give all your worries and cares to God, for he cares about you. (1 Peter 5:7 NLT)

† Do not fear, for I am with you; do not be afraid, for I am your God. I will strengthen you; I will help you; I will hold on to you with My righteous right hand. (Isaiah 41:10 CSB)

† In my distress I called to the Lord; he answered me and set me free. The Lord is with me, I will not be afraid; what can anyone do to me? (Psalms 118:5-6 GNT)

† If then God so clothe the grass, which is today in the field, and tomorrow is cast into the oven; how much more will he clothe you, O ye of little faith? And seek not ye what ye shall eat, or what ye shall drink, neither be ye of doubtful mind. For all these things do the nations of the world seek after: and your Father knoweth that ye have need of these things. (Luke 12:28-30 KJV)

† Do not be anxious about anything, but in every situation, by prayer and petition, with thanksgiving, present your requests to God. And the peace of God, which transcends all understanding, will guard your hearts and your minds in Christ Jesus. (Philippians 4:6-7 NIV)

† So do not worry about tomorrow; for tomorrow will worry about itself. Each day has enough trouble of its own. (Matthew 6:34 LSB)

† In my distress I called upon the Lord; to my God I cried

for help. From his temple he heard my voice, and my cry to him reached his ears. (Psalm 18:6 CSB)

✝ Therefore I say unto you, Take no thought for your life, what ye shall eat, or what ye shall drink; nor yet for your body, what ye shall put on. Is not the life more than meat, and the body than raiment? Behold the fowls of the air: for they sow not, neither do they reap, nor gather into barns; yet your heavenly Father feedeth them. Are ye not much better than they? (Matthew 6:25-26 KJV)

✝ But blessed are those who trust in the LORD and have made the LORD their hope and confidence. They are like trees planted along a riverbank, with roots that reach deep into the water. Such trees are not bothered by the heat or worried by long months of drought. Their leaves stay green, and they never stop producing fruit. (Jerimiah 17:7-8 NLT)

# Chapter 5

## *Addicted to Love*

*It's closer to the truth to say you can't get enough.*
*You're gonna have to face it, you're addicted to love.*

— Robert Palmer

I entered the tenth grade feeling isolated; I had no friends and was going through the motions trying to graduate from high school. The situation at home hadn't changed, and in some ways, it worsened partly because Brenda incessantly complained to me about my dad drinking and was over-the-top obsessed with George, which drove my dad further away from her. Dad rarely spoke to me and spent most of his time drinking in the "shop," he had built behind the house. I felt hollow and miserable and longed for the day when I could escape the confines in which I lived.

I was incessantly lonely and desperately missed Alex. Life without him was unbearable, and I became intensely driven to fill the emptiness inside me; to feel loved again. I didn't realize it then, but the emotional neglect I experienced throughout my childhood precipitated an insatiable need to be loved that would dominate my life for the next forty-five years. Being loved became an obsession. I would become whomever I needed to be, fix whatever problem needed to be fixed, repair the brokenness, or be the caregiver. Whatever it took to be "loved," I would do it, and it always ended in despair and to my detriment. Over the next forty-five years, I would marry and divorce seven times and would have a number of relationships between marriages. I couldn't bear to be alone, and as Robert Palmer sang, I was "addicted to love," and it controlled my life as much as alcohol or heroin would.

## Husband #1

Jerry was my first husband. We met when I was a sophomore in high school. Jerry was a junior and drove a souped-up Plymouth Duster in cherry condition. We began to date and I soon felt the emptiness inside me subside. The love I felt for Jerry didn't come close to the love I felt for Alex, and that would be the case with all of my relationships for the rest of my life. I would never know love to that depth and with that completeness ever again. I would forever settle for love that was good enough. Good enough to quench the thirst sufficient to sustain life but never overflowing.

Jerry and I dated for about six months before we dropped out of high school and got married. I loved Jerry, but in the back of my mind, I knew I was getting married partially to get out of the black hole I was living in. It was my ticket out of the house and a chance to live my own life.

Brenda didn't bat an eye when I told her I wanted to get married and gave her consent without first consulting my dad. She was probably relieved and jumping for joy because I would finally be out of her hair.

Jerry and I were married about a month later. I don't remember the date or month we got married, but it must have been during late winter or early spring because my wedding dress was long-sleeved, and instead of a veil, I wore a hooded cape trimmed with white faux fur. I saw the dress in a magazine and fell in love with it, so Brenda had a seamstress reproduce it for me. For Brenda to do something that special for me was a sure sign that she was as happy I was getting married as I was. I don't remember much about the wedding, only that it was in a Lutheran church and very few people attended. I don't even remember having a wedding reception, but I do remember feeling like I had just escaped prison.

After we were married, we rented a double-wide trailer and furnished it with items friends and family had given us or we purchased from second-hand stores. I got a job as a cashier at a gas station and Jerry worked at an auto repair shop as a mechanic. I loved living life on my own terms and living it with someone who loved me, but after three short months, I knew I had made a huge mistake. Jerry had six jobs during the first three months we were married and was caught stealing from his last employer.

It wasn't because Jerry couldn't hold down a job or that we were relying on his parents to eat and keep a roof over our heads that I ended the marriage. I had been in this space before when I ran away from home and knew what it was like to wonder where my next meal was coming from. I was ready and willing to do whatever I could to get us through it, but when Jerry stole money from his employer, that was my hard stop.

Now I know marriage is supposed to be forever, in sickness and health, for richer or poorer, until death do us part. And, I know many people have stood by their spouse when they have done things that were much worse than stealing from their employer, but I couldn't get over it. To me, it was inexcusable. Jerry had crossed the line, and it was something I couldn't accept or live with.

## Divorced at Sixteen

When I decided to divorce Jerry, I had no money or car, only my job at the gas station. I was so desperate for a place to live that I called Brenda and asked her if I could come back home to live until I could get on my feet. Brenda rejected the prospect and said, "No, I don't think you could live by the rules of this house." She didn't offer to help me in any way and seemed glad to be rid of me for good. I hung up the phone in disbelief that she would rather I lived on the streets than have me live in her house again. This was the final cut, and it was to the bone. I felt so unloved, rejected, and alone. I became driven to survive and to show Brenda and my dad that I didn't need them and never would.

Jerry moved back home to his parent's house, and I managed to scrape together the money I needed to rent a small apartment within walking distance of my job. It wasn't much, but it was clean and cheap. I got another full-time job as a waitress at a western restaurant where they served rocky mountain oysters and spent most of my working time rejecting the advances of the urban cowboy patrons. Even with two full-time jobs, money was tight. The gas station paid minimum wage, and the restaurant paid less than that, so I had to rely heavily on the tips I made, which were never consistent. Most of my money went toward rent and utilities, and any surplus I had, I used to buy groceries. One month, grocery money was so scarce I purchased enough ingredients to make banana bread for the entire month, only having to go to the store each week to buy fresh bananas.

This was definitely one of the low points of my life. I was sixteen years old, broke, divorced, a high school dropout, working two full-time jobs, didn't have a car or driver's license, and had no friends or family. Life was hard, but I was still happier living under these conditions than I had ever been living at home. I became independent, a survivor, and learned to rely solely on myself. I had to learn to navigate through life on my own. I learned how to do laundry, cook, file my taxes, ride the bus, pay bills, open a bank account, write checks, budget money, drive, and buy and maintain a car. After two years of barely making ends meet working two to three jobs at a time as a hostess, waitress, cashier, or fast food cook, I got a General Education Degree (GED). Obtaining a GED was one of the best decisions I made, as it not only opened doors for higher-paying jobs, but it made it possible for me to further my education in the future.

## Husband #2

My girlfriend, Betty, and I got jobs at a truss manufacturer. We usually worked on an assembly line securing truss plates onto truss joints using a large nail gun, but sometimes we worked in the yard, banding together groups of 16'- 40' high trusses using a metal strapping tool. The work was hard, but it paid more than I had been making working two jobs, so I considered it a godsend.

I met Matt when we worked a shift together on the same assembly line. We started hanging out together on our breaks and at a bar a few blocks from the plant, where many workers would go after work to wind down. Matt's brother-in-law, Troy, was a foreman at the plant and would spend much of his time in the office that was encased in glass and sat high above the assembly lines, giving him a bird's eye view of the entire operation.

Matt and Troy were close friends and would hang out in the office during working hours for long periods of time. Considering the relationship, no one dared complain about Matt spending time in the office with Troy instead of working with the rest of the workers in the plant. It wasn't until Matt and I started dating that I learned Troy was a heavy cocaine (coke) user, and he and Matt would spend their time up in the office doing lines, sometimes accompanied by a whiskey chaser. When Matt and I started dating, he used coke, but not at the level that Troy did. Troy's wife, Jan, also used coke, and like Matt, didn't use it to the extent that Troy did. Before dating Matt, I had used various drugs, including coke, so I fit right into their cocaine clan.

After about three months of dating, Matt and I moved into an apartment and lived together for about six months before we got married. We were happy for the first two years of our marriage. We loved each other, were financially stable, and had the love and support of Matt's family who had accepted me as one of their own. I had finally found the love I had so desperately longed for.

By the third year of our marriage, Matt's coke habit had increased significantly, but not nearly as much as Troy's had. Troy started to shoot coke, and it got to the point where it was rare to see Troy when he wasn't high. I never saw him shoot up at work, but there were plenty of times when I went to the office, and he and Matt would be up there doing lines. We all saw Troy going downhill fast, but when we would say something to him about it he would immediately reject our advice and tell us he had everything under control. We knew he didn't. Not even close.

Like most Saturday nights, Jan and Troy came to our apartment to hang out, drink beer, and get high. We sat around the dining room table in our usual seats: Matt and I sat on one side of the table, Troy sat across from me, and Jan sat across from Matt. We would begin our ritual by pouring a small pile of coke onto a mirror and carefully dividing it into several thin, parallel lines. We did so with quick precision that only comes from performing a task hundreds of times before.

After snorting several rounds of lines and drinking a few more beers, Troy reached into his backpack, pulled out a small, brown pouch and carefully placed it on the table. We all watched as Troy purposefully arranged his "shooting kit" as if he were a surgeon arranging instruments in preparation for surgery. When the coke had been cooked to his liking, Troy drew the liquid into a needle filtering it through a small piece of cotton, tapped the barrel, and carefully pushed the plunger, removing the air bubbles from the solution. Troy skillfully tied a tourniquet around his left upper arm and tied it off, exposing a well-used vein.

With great anticipation, Troy slowly injected the liquid into the protruding vein in his arm. Before Troy could remove the tourniquet, his eyes rolled to the back of his head, and he began to convulse violently. As the twisting and jerky contortions of his body ended, he slipped into unconsciousness and fell to the floor. Matt ran over to Troy, picked him up, and carried him to the couch. Jan was crying hysterically while yelling at Troy and shaking his unresponsive body in a futile attempt to revive him. Matt and I quickly and frantically disposed of the coke and paraphernalia before calling 911, hoping to lessen the retribution that was sure to come when the police arrived on an overdose call.

My heart was beating out of my chest as I watched one EMT strap Troy to the gurney while the other EMT performed CPR. I must have been in shock because I could hear myself answering the questions the police officer was asking me, but it felt like I was having an out-of-body experience, observing but not really there. It was like a bad dream I knew I was having, but from which I couldn't wake myself up.

The police officers followed the EMTs as they exited the apartment and hurriedly loaded Troy into the ambulance. After several minutes of following the ambulance to the hospital, the lights and sirens suddenly shut off. When Jan saw this, she shouted, "Why did they shut the lights and siren off? What does that mean? Does that mean Troy is dead?" Matt and I responded silently, hoping Jan wasn't correct in her deduction. We would later learn she had been.

Matt and I moved out of the apartment and rented a house with Matt's younger brother. Jan was grief-stricken by Troy's death and resigned herself from life. Matt buried his grief in coke and began freebasing. I followed Matt down the freebasing hell hole and watched it quickly devour us and our lives. Freebasing was a process used in the 1970s through the 1990s where ether was used to separate any impurities and additives from the cocaine, making the base of the cocaine into a smokable substance. Crack cocaine replaced freebasing, as using a lighter with a substance purified with ether was a disaster waiting to happen (no one ever said freebasers were smart)[1].

Freebasing enabled one to obtain the ultimate high without shooting it. The rush from freebasing hooked me the first time I tried it. When you snort cocaine, the high is less intense than freebasing and peaks after about 30 - 60 minutes. When you freebase, the fierce rush hits you in a few seconds and then subsides into a state of euphoria that lasts about fifteen minutes (twenty minutes if you're lucky). Freebasing is so addictive, I liken it to the Lays potato chips slogan: no one can eat (hit) just one (once). One hit of freebase can lead to an entire night of freebasing. Essentially, you smoked it until there was none left because you couldn't stop on your own.

Freebasing only on the weekends quickly snowballed into smoking it almost every night, and if we had enough cocaine, we would freebase for days on end. Freebasing had its hooks in us so deep it became our reason for living. It got to the point where we were spending so much on cocaine that we were having a hard time paying our bills. The ah-ha moment for me was when I answered the door one day, and a guy I'd never seen before asked me if Matt was home. I told him he wasn't, and he told me to tell him that he wanted the money Matt owed him by the following day.

When Matt came home, I questioned him about the visitor who claimed Matt owed him money. Matt came clean and told me he had been selling cocaine to pay our bills (oh, but wait, it gets better). Matt then told me we had freebased all of the cocaine he was supposed to sell, and he didn't have the money to pay the guy what he owed him. I immediately envisioned the drug dealer showing up at our door the next day to collect his money, accompanied by two WWA wrestlers carrying baseball bats. We had hit rock bottom, and Matt was digging our graves. It was then that I decided I was done. Done with freebasing and done with Matt.

When I got up the next morning, Matt was gone. I found a note he'd left for me that said he was out trying to get enough money to pay off the dealer. This was my chance. My chance to leave this life behind and get straight. I called Betty, told her what Matt had done, and told her I wanted to leave him. We devised a plan to sell whatever we could to raise enough money to move to California. Betty and I didn't waste any time. We rented a U-Haul trailer that day, loaded it and my car with everything we owned, and went to a flea market where we sold our belongings and made enough money to get us to California. My freebasing days were over, and so were my days with Matt.

## Reflection of Hope

We push so hard through life, trying to make it turn out as we had envisioned. It rarely does. I thought marrying Jerry was my ticket to freedom. I could finally live life my way with someone who loved me. And then life happened. We believe we have so much control over our lives, and if we do X, we will have Y. I have news for you. There are twenty-four other letters that have a will of their own that will inevitably come in and kick Y out the door. So, how do we handle this madness we call life? We stop trying to swim against the tide and instead swim with it.

As I reflect on who I was during this time, I can see things much more clearly and better understand the purpose of it all. I see that there are infinite possibilities and that a small deviation can change the entire portrait of our life. As a child, I was astounded by the beauty of the ever-changing patterns created by the turns of a kaleidoscope. I didn't understand how it worked, but I didn't need to in order to appreciate the complexity and uniqueness of the images that were created.

Through a combination of light, mirrors, objects, and angles, every movement of a kaleidoscope produces a pattern that occurs only once and can never be replicated. When light enters a kaleidoscope, it is reflected and redirected by the mirrors and objects within it, producing the unique colors, shapes, designs, and patterns[2].

In some ways, we are similar to a kaleidoscope in that we come into this world equipped with our own distinct set of mirrors and a fixed number of objects that move freely within us. As we move through life, we reflect and redirect light to create the unique designs and patterns of our lives that only occur once and can never be changed.

We only have control over our movements and the light within us. We cannot control the free-flowing, colorful objects that welcome the light and fall where they will. They cannot be controlled, however hard we try. We must accept the patterns and designs we create and see the beauty in them even when the image turns out to be contrary to what we had in mind.

Life is the attitude we choose to have. When we fall, we have a choice to make. Will we sit there and wallow in our mess, kicking and screaming and blaming everyone but ourselves because our butt is in the dirt? Will we sit there waiting for someone to pick us up and, as we wait, never consider how we got there? Or will we sit there for a minute, enjoy the beauty around us, and be grateful we didn't break a bone? Will we get up and dust ourselves off and not repeat the mistake that put us on the ground to begin with? The choice is ours to make.

Coming home has freed me from life's turmoil. I now live my life for God rather than living it for my selfish wants and desires. To some of you, this may seem counterintuitive. You may say, "Of course I'm going to live my life for myself. It's my life. Who else am I going to live it for?" This is how I've lived my life until about four months ago, and, in many ways, it has not served me well. You must find your why, your reason for being. This is not an easy thing to do. You must dig deep, very deep. Before coming home, my why was desperately searching for a man to love me. Every breath I took and every choice I made was done with only one thing in mind: to feel loved. The problem was I was searching for the wrong kind of love.

God loves us for who we are. God's love is unconditional, whereas human love always comes with conditions. God's love is as vast as the heavens and is unfailing (Psalm 36:5-7 NLT). What kind of a God still loves me when I have cursed him? What kind of a God protects me when I have denied His existence? And, what kind of a God provides for me when I have turned my back on Him? I had turned my back on God, and what did he do in return? He protected me from danger when I would walk home from work in the darkness of the night. He always provided for me. I never went hungry and always had a roof over my head and enough money to pay my bills. He protected me from overdosing like Troy did and made it possible for me to walk away from freebasing. He did all of this for me after I pushed him away. I didn't deserve any of it, but God didn't give up on me and was always watching over me.

God is the light shining into my kaleidoscope, showing me where I am needed and who he wants me to help and love. I don't question my commissions; I praise God for them because this gives me a chance to love and be loved in a way only those who come home can understand. It is liberating and frees me from my worries as I turn them all over to God and let Him take care of them or receive the strength from Him that I need to persevere. I pray you will let God be the light in your kaleidoscope and witness the magnificence in how he orchestrates your life. And, I pray Jesus becomes your why, as He has become mine.

## Scriptures of Hope

✝ But let all who take refuge in you rejoice; let them sing joyful praises forever.

Spread your protection over them, that all who love your name may be filled with joy.
For you bless the godly, O LORD; you surround them with your shield of love. (Psalm 5:11-12 NLT)

✝ Thy mercy, O LORD, is in the heavens; and thy faithfulness reacheth unto the clouds.
Thy righteousness is like the great mountains; thy judgments are a great deep: O LORD, thou preservest man and beast.
How excellent is thy loving kindness, O God! therefore the children of men put their trust under the shadow of thy wings. (Psalm 36:5-7 KJV)

✝ Behold what manner of love the Father has bestowed on us, that we should be called children of God! Therefore the world does not know us, because it did not know Him. (1 John 3:1 NKJV)

✝ For God so loved the world, that he gave his only Son, that whoever believes in him should not perish but have eternal life. (John 3:16 ESV)

✝ But God proves his own love for us in that while we were still sinners, Christ died for us. (Romans 5:8 CSB)

✝ Either way, Christ's love controls us. Since we believe that Christ died for all, we also believe that we have all died to our old life. He died for everyone so that those who receive his new life will no longer live for themselves. Instead, they will live for Christ, who died and was raised for them. (2 Corinthians 5:14-15 NLT)

✝ The steadfast love of the LORD never ceases;
his mercies never come to an end;
they are new every morning;
great is thy faithfulness. (Lamentations 3:22-23 ESV)

✝ Be strong and courageous. Do not fear or be in dread of them, for it is the Lord your God who goes with you. He will not leave you or forsake you. (Deuteronomy 31:6 ESV)

✝ And we know that in all things God works for the good of those who love him, who have been called according to his purpose. (Romans 8:28 NIV)

✝ So Jesus was saying to those Jews who had believed Him, "If you abide in My word, then you are truly My disciples; and you will know the truth, and the truth will make you free. (John 8:31-32 LSB)

# Chapter 6

## *Shoes on Their Feet*

*I've never loved anybody the way I love my children.*

— Katey Sagal

The move to California was more like a three-month spring break party. We sold everything we brought to the flea market and loaded the remaining items into the small U-Haul trailer hitched to the back of my 1972 canary yellow Chevy Camaro Z28. It was summertime, and we began our trip anticipating a fresh start and a new life. On the way, we stopped at a small mining town to go to the bathroom, get some fuel, and grab something quick to eat. The town was engaged in some sort of annual summer celebration with games, booths with merchants displaying their wares, and plenty of country-style food.

As Betty and I wandered through the festivities, we came upon a mucking contest where the first-place prize was one hundred dollars. We approached a woman sitting at a card table who was in charge of registering contestants and asked her what a mucking contest was and what you had to do to win first prize. She explained that a large pile of dirt and rocks had to be shoveled from one side of a divider to the other, and the team that shoveled the most dirt and rocks to the other side in two minutes won first prize. Large, burly men looked on, snickering under their breath as Betty and I signed up for the contest; two of them, I'm sure, were the defending champions.

Including Betty and I, there were a total of three teams participating in the competition. Betty and I watched as the first team of brawny men impressively shoveled about half of the pile of dirt in the allotted time, and we began to wonder if we had signed up for something that was way out of our league. The second team of hulk-like men took their positions, each with a smug look of confidence on their face. They effortlessly shoveled about two-thirds of the pile to the other side of the divider in the allotted time and walked away with confidence that they had claimed the title of mucking champions. Betty and I looked at the enormous pile of dirt they had shoveled and came close to conceding but decided, "What the hell. Let's do this."

Betty and I approached our pile of dirt and took the same positions the previous two teams had taken, facing each other on opposite sides of the box. With shovels in hand, the starting bell rang and for two minutes, Betty and I mucked our hearts out, not even taking time to look over to the other side to assess our progress. When the bell rang, indicating our time was up, we knew we hadn't shoveled the entire pile of dirt to the other side, but as we looked over to see our accomplishment, we immediately knew we had beaten the other two teams.

Everyone, including us, was astounded and stared at our winning dirt pile in disbelief. There was no good-job clapping or celebratory hoots and hollers from the audience. Just a shaking of heads as they silently walked away in humiliation. With ear-to-ear grins, Betty and I walked over to the lady sitting behind the card table to collect our winnings. She didn't say anything to us, but we noticed the smirk on her face as if to say, "Damn, that was fun watching two women kick those guys' butts. I can't wait to spread this news all around town."

We made it as far as Las Vegas when my car broke down. Betty and I rode with the tow truck driver to the auto repair shop, wondering what this mishap would cost us and if we would have enough money to pay for the repairs. It was late in the day when we arrived at the repair shop; too late to get the needed parts, leaving us no choice but to spend the night. We found the cheapest motel room within walking distance of the repair shop.

The room was small and reminded me of a motel room you might see in a slasher movie. It looked more like a large bathroom than a bedroom with 1970s pale blue bathroom tile covering the floor, graffitied walls, and stained floral curtains that would flutter when an occasional breeze would find its way through the hole in the window. The only furniture in the room was a single bed with no headboard that was made up with sheets and a thin cotton blanket. The saving grace about the room was it was roach-free, which more than made up for the brown rings in the toilet.

The next morning, Betty and I went to the repair shop to

get an idea of when the repairs would be completed and what it would cost to get us on the road again. We had been frugal with our flea market money and our mucking contest winnings, but if the repairs were significant, we'd be stuck staying in the slasher movie room until we could raise the money we needed to get to California.

As Betty and I approached the repair shop, we saw my car in the bay with the lower half of two oil-stained, blue jean covered legs and boots sticking out from underneath it. We announced that we were there and asked the mechanic if he had determined the source of the problem. We waited for him to push himself out on the creeper from underneath the car to give us the bad news, but instead he yelled, "Looks like you ran over a rabbit. It's all over the undercarriage." Another mechanic walking into the bay chuckled at the remark and we both turned to him and gave him a "not-funny" look. Noticing we were not amused, he lost his sarcastic smile and began explaining what was wrong with my car and what the cost would be to repair it. Our pocketbook took a hit, but we had enough to cover the repairs and get us the rest of the way to California.

I loved the ocean and had always wanted to live in California, so when I saw the "Welcome to California" sign on the side of the highway, I let out a big "Oowee" and cranked up the rock-n-roll. San Diego was sunny and beautiful. I felt as if I had died and gone to heaven and was very excited to start my new life there. We checked into a cheap hotel room that was like the Taj Mahal compared to the slasher movie room we had in Las Vegas. It was clean, had two fully made-up beds with headboards, and had no brown rings in the toilet. Betty and I settled into our room and then wasted no time making our way to the swimming pool, fully equipped with beach towels and sunscreen.

We spent the next three months partying–not looking for jobs or a place to live, just jumping from one party to the next, never staying at any one place for more than a few days. It was a wild ride, and as all things eventually do, our stay in California came to an end when the parties ran dry and we realized we were broke and homeless. Betty and I decided to return to Colorado, so with U-Haul in tow, we headed home.

We made it to Colorado but ran out of gas about fifty miles from Betty's parents' house, where we planned to stay until we could get a place of our own. As we sat in the car pondering how we would get the gas we needed, I remembered I had packed away a change jar in the U-Haul. So, there we were, on the side of the road, rummaging through the U-Haul in a desperate attempt to locate the change jar.

After about ten minutes of searching, Betty yelled, "I found it." as she held up the empty change jar. An empty jar meant only one thing. It had fallen over, and our precious change had scattered all over the floor of the U-Haul. I'm sure it was a sight to see, both of us systematically unloading the U-Haul while keeping our eyes peeled for the life-saving pennies, nickels, dimes, and quarters that would get us to our final destination.

We ended our search at the end of the better part of an hour when we realized we had probably found the majority of the change. We sat on the open end of the U-Haul, carefully poured the change into a pile, and began to count what felt like Las Vegas winnings. With the change jar in hand, Betty and I hitchhiked to the nearest gas station, borrowed a gas can, filled it with gas, and hitchhiked back to my car.

After about six months, Betty and I parted ways. Actually, it was me who parted ways from Betty. Betty was one of those friends who did nothing but drag you down the road to nowhere with them. Her life consisted of getting drunk and high and leeching off of anyone and everyone. I had had enough. I wanted more out of life and wanted to make something out of myself.

I got my own apartment and enrolled in the computer science program at a community college. I left the restaurant industry and got a job working in the office at the warehouse of an office supply company. It was an entry-level clerical job, but I soon worked my way up to a position as the assistant to the sales manager. Working a full-time job and carrying a full load of classes at the community college was hard, but I was determined to be successful and make a good life for myself.

I made friends with the computer programmer and operator who would occasionally emerge from the computer room upstairs to confer with their manager, whose office was across the hall from the sales office where I worked. On some days, I would go upstairs to the computer room during my lunch hour to visit my friends. I was enthralled with the two ginormous mainframe computers running in the temperature-controlled room, the magnetic tape capturing the day's data, and the buzzing sound of the massive reports feeding through the dot matrix printer.

It took about a year, but my hard work finally paid off when an entry-level computer operator position became available and I was able to leave the sales department and begin a new career in the computer industry, which I hoped would lead to a computer programming position. I was about halfway through the computer science program and had found my passion to be in computer programming. In those days, the predominant computer languages were BASIC and FORTRAN, both of which I had been learning in school. The computer programmer took me under his wing and began tutoring me through troubleshooting programming bugs and creating entry-level computer programs.

Outside, on the fringe of the back parking lot, a large computer backup generator stood by to provide power to the mainframe computers should we experience a power outage. The company that supplied the backup generator was a family-owned business located in Utah. Each quarter, one of the owners would travel to our location to perform preventative maintenance on the generator. It was on one of these occasions when I met my third husband, Kyle.

Kyle was the oldest of three children who were co-owners of the company with their parents. I met Kyle in June when he flew the company's small fixed-wing plane to Colorado to service the backup generator. Kyle was handsome, brilliant, witty, and was the cornerstone of the family's successful business. I was awestruck by Kyle and thrilled when he invited my supervisor, Brock, and me to a Fourth of July Lake Powell outing he and his family had planned. Kyle would pick up Brock and me in the company plane at a small airport outside of Denver and we would fly to Lake Powell, where we would rendezvous with his family. His parents would stay in their oversized motorhome and the rest of us would camp on the shore. Kyle had a large speedboat that we would use to water ski and explore the lake and canyons.

I was beside myself, waiting for Kyle to land. He was late, and even though we hadn't spent much time together, I was worried sick, pacing up and down the small airport. The airport attendant told us Kyle had run into some unexpected bad weather and was going to be late. How late, she didn't know. That depended on how bad the weather turned. After about an hour past his scheduled arrival time, Brock and I finally saw Kyle walking toward the airport building.

"Whew. Ran into some weather on the way over," Kyle said excitedly as he walked through the door, grinning from ear to ear.

"I was worried sick!" I exclaimed.

"Aw, nothing to worry about. I had a blast up there."

I could only shake my head at Kyle and his dismissiveness of the obvious danger. To him, it was thrilling and challenging. To me, it was terrifying.

We loaded our bags on the plane. Fortunately, we were traveling away from the storm into clear skies. About thirty minutes into the flight, Kyle turned to me and asked me what I thought about flying in a small plane. When I told Kyle I thought it was a little boring, he grinned devilishly and immediately turned the plane over on its side. I could hear Brock yell out a "Whoa" from the back seat, as we began to fall from the sky. My eyes became as large as saucers and my knuckles became white as I gripped the armrests in terror.

Kyle began to laugh as he maneuvered the plane from side to side.

"Boring, huh? Are you bored now?" Kyle asked, smiling and thoroughly enjoying his prank.

We arrived late in the afternoon, not having time to do much but set up camp and do a little water skiing. That night, Kyle, Brock, and I fell asleep in Kyle's speedboat that we had beached on the shore near camp. I was awakened in the middle of the night by water splashing in my ear. As I awoke, I saw that about two inches of water had accumulated inside the boat and was sloshing back and forth to the rhythm of the waves lapping on the shore. I woke Kyle and Brock and informed them of my discovery and they immediately jumped into action.

Our excitement woke those sleeping on the shore and they rushed over to see what was going on. Kyle took charge and told everyone to start bailing the water out of the boat before it sank. Everyone grabbed whatever they could find that would hold water and began bailing water out of the sinking boat. It took about twenty minutes, but we finally got ahead of it and removed enough water from the boat to where it was light enough to push it further onto the shore to keep it from sinking. Until then, it was all hands on deck, go time, and serious business, but after the boat was safely on the shore, everyone breathed a sigh of relief and busted out laughing.

The next two days were as eventful as the first day had been. We spent the time rock climbing, water skiing, and exploring deep into the canyons until the boat could no longer move forward and we could touch the canyon walls. It was a time full of adventure and, for Kyle and me, a time to fall in love. Two months later, Kyle and I got married in Colorado and I moved to Utah. I got a job as a computer operator at a steel company, and six months later, I was pregnant with our first child. Kyle and I hadn't planned on having any children, but when I got pregnant while using an IUD for birth control, we decided I would have the IUD removed and if the baby survived and there were no complications with the pregnancy, we would keep it.

Our daughter was born ten months later, perfectly healthy and with no adverse effects experienced during the pregnancy. I'm not sure if the doctor miscalculated the birth date or if she was truly born a month late, but after eleven hours of labor and only dilating to three cm, my doctor made the call to perform a cesarean section. Before giving birth, I had quit my job at the steel company and went to work at Kyle's family's business. I worked accounts receivable and any other odd job that needed to be done. When I joined the company, Kyle's entire family worked there, including his brother's wife and his sister's husband.

Two and a half years later, Kyle and I had another daughter. This time, it was intentional, and she would be the last child I would have. Two years later, I graduated with a bachelor's degree in business administration with a minor in operations management. Life was good. We were happy working in the family business, which was flourishing, or so we thought.

Kyle and I were in Colorado working at one of the generator sites when Kyle received a call from his mother. She called to tell him the IRS was at the office and was shutting down the company because they owed a large amount of payroll taxes. Kyle and I were flabbergasted. When we returned home, we learned that Kyle's sister, who was in charge of payroll and the general accounting of the company, hadn't paid payroll taxes to the IRS for the last several years. My suspicion was that Kyle's mother, who was the president of the company, was in cahoots with his sister because the company was having a cash flow problem and this was a way to stay afloat.

In one fell swoop, the entire family and other employees were out of a job. Kyle and I should have seen this coming when we hadn't received paychecks for the last couple of months. When Kyle confronted his mother about it, she assured him the company was solid and they were expecting a large payment on one of the generators "any day now." But the nightmare didn't end there for Kyle and me. Kyle and his father had the same first name but different middle names, and when the company shut down, his parents allowed his father's debt to fall to Kyle. Needless to say, the whole ordeal forced Kyle and me to sever the relationship with his parents, his sister, and his brother-in-law.

Kyle and I sold the boat and other assets to pay bills and survive until we could get our own company up and running. Kyle picked up the preventative maintenance contracts from the defunct family business, which saw us through until we could sell a backup generator. Kyle expanded the business by selling control panels and providing generator systems for purposes other than backup power for mainframe computers. We secured a small business loan and purchased a small piece of property with a house and a shop on it. I handled the accounting and the business side of things, while Kyle handled the manufacturing and fieldwork. Within two years, we had built a successful business that was operating in the black. And then it wasn't.

The "shop" was a large wooden structure behind the house that we used as an office. All the tools and equipment were housed in the shop where the manufacturing occurred. One warm summer day, as I was working in the office, I looked out of the window and saw smoke pouring out of the shop and employees fleeing from the building. It didn't take but a few minutes before the structure and everything in it was destroyed. Thankfully, no one was hurt, but it was a disaster from which we couldn't recover financially, which left us no choice but to close the business and sell the property.

I got a job as a police officer with a local police department and Kyle kept the business open working the preventative maintenance contracts we had on the generators. Kyle wanted to expand the business by designing and building control panels. He was obsessed with keeping the business alive. But, even with me working full time and Kyle working what little remained from the business, we were drowning in debt and couldn't financially keep our heads above water.

"I want to keep the company going. Having my own business is my dream," Kyle said.

We had been fighting about the same issue for weeks. I wanted Kyle to close the company and get a job. The fights became more heated and the girls would huddle together in fear in the corner of one of their bedrooms as Kyle and I shouted at one another. One night, as we were in the kitchen fighting, Kyle threw a dish at a wall in an effort to be heard and demonstrate the passion of his position.

"You need to get a real job with a steady paycheck," I demanded.

"We can't even afford to put shoes on our children's feet and you want to keep working in the business?"

It was at this point that I told Kyle to choose between his dream and his family. Kyle chose his dream. The way I saw it, Kyle was willing to forgo his family's needs in order to have his own business. This was not alright with me. Kyle and I had been married for nine years and had been through a lot together, but I never thought I'd see the day when he would turn his back on his children. As I examined our lives and our future as a family, I didn't really want to go through another divorce, especially now that we had children.

*Isn't it better to keep the family together where our children have both parents? Do I want to have another failed marriage? We can get through this, can't we? I can't believe Kyle has chosen his work over his family. Is it better for our children to live in an environment where they are living in fear, seeing their parents arguing and yelling at each other every night or to live in an environment where the parents are divorced and there is peace? Do I want my girls to grow up thinking this is a "normal" marriage and have them get involved in relationships where fighting is the norm and becomes their comfort zone?*

After much contemplation, I chose divorce with peace. I wanted my girls to see that this was not how a marriage should be and that what was happening was unacceptable. I didn't want them to follow suit and marry someone who didn't put them and their children above all else. I know many people stay together because they don't want to break up the family and want their children to live in a two-parent household, but I don't think that is always the best thing for children. We must teach our children that they are valued and show them that we love them enough to remove them from a horrible situation, one that could alter their lives for the worse. Sometimes, divorcing is the right thing to do.

## Reflection of Hope

You must keep climbing the mountain because the higher you go, the more you can see. If we look back on our lives, we would probably see a series of roller coasters that we kept standing in line for. Why do we keep standing in line? Because it's fun? Sometimes. We keep standing in line for love; love of friends, love of family, love of ourselves. With love, there is hope. And, when there is hope, there is another day.

As I look back at my rollercoasters, I can't help but notice the pattern of lows and highs. I don't know about you, but my life has been, and will always be, a series of lows and highs. It's the momentum of life that carries us through. We don't have control over the unique twists and turns of the roller coaster we are riding, but most of the time, we have a choice of which roller coaster we are going to ride.

When I left Matt, I looked at my options of roller coasters and decided I wanted to ride on the one that was exciting, new, and full of adventure. So, what did I do? I sold practically everything I owned and went to California. Boy, that was a bumpy ride. But, do you notice (maybe we all need to take time to notice) that at the end of the ride, you are level and have come to a stop and have received blessings along the way?

The change jar was a blessing when we were stuck on the side of the road. My girls were my blessings when Kyle and I divorced. We need to focus on our blessings, as they are gifts that have been given to us. They are your most valuable possessions. God watches over us and makes sure we have plenty of blessings and all of the things we need to keep going and get on another ride. It is easy to focus on our troubles and pain. They will consume us if we allow them to.

We need to take notice of and focus on our blessings. There is at least one blessing in every situation, even if we don't see it at the time. And, if we don't see it, it could be we're not looking hard enough or looking at all. When you focus on your blessings rather than your troubles and pain, you begin to feel your heart lift and get a sense that everything is going to be okay. It makes you think more clearly and objectively. It can take you out of panic mode.

I take notice of my blessings and give thanks every day for the bounty the Lord has bestowed upon me. With every blessing I add to the list, I am lifted a little higher up above my troubles, which makes me realize how fortunate I am. Try it now. Think of a problem you are having or something that isn't going right in your life. Now, take five minutes and list in your head or on paper all of your blessings and everything you are grateful for. I guarantee you will have at least ten blessings on your list, probably more, and your problem will have shrunk in size.

Here are the top blessings on my list:

1. I'm home with God,
2. my church,
3. family (each family member counts as one blessing),
4. friends,
5. my job,
6. my pets,
7. my health,
8. the food I have in the kitchen,
9. my home,
10. and this day.

Blessings are the air you breathe, the rose bush in your yard, nature, all of your possessions, the love in your life, the beauty around you, and so on. Counting your blessings is a form of prayer. It's taking the time to let God know you appreciate everything and everyone He has given to you to enjoy and cherish while you are on this earth.

Another surefire way to shrink your troubles down to size is to give them up to God. That doesn't mean you don't do what you can to solve the problem. It means you let God worry about it. Do what you can, and don't worry about things you have no control over. God will provide. God will carry us through. God will love us, always. God will always be holding your hand every step of the way.

## Scriptures of Hope

✝ Don't worry about anything; instead, pray about everything.

Tell God what you need, and thank him for all he has done. Then you will experience God's peace, which exceeds anything we can understand. His peace will guard your hearts and minds as you live in Christ Jesus. (Philippians 4: 6-7 NLT).

✝ "Fear not, for I am with you; Be not dismayed, for I am your God. I will strengthen you, Yes, I will help you, I will uphold you with My righteous right hand." (Isaiah 41:10 NKJV).

✝ Casting all your anxieties on him, because he cares for you. (1 Peter 5:7 NIV).

✝ Cast your burden on the Lord, and he will sustain you; he will never permit the righteous to be moved. (Psalm 55:22 ESV).

✝ I can do all things through him who strengthens me. Philippians 4:13 CSB).

✝ Ask, and it will be given to you; seek, and you will find; knock, and it will be opened to you. For everyone who asks receives, and the one who seeks finds, and to the one who knocks it will be opened. (Matthew 7:7-8 KJV).

✝ Do not be anxious about anything, but in everything by prayer and supplication with thanksgiving let your requests be made known to God. (Philippians 4:6 NKJV).

✝ For I, the Lord your God, hold your right hand; it is I who say to you, "Fear not, I am the one who helps you." (Isaiah 41:13 ESV).

✝ In their hearts humans plan their course, but the LORD establishes their steps. (Proverbs 16:9 NIV).

✝ "Call on me in a day of trouble; I will rescue you, and you will honor me." (Psalm 50:15 CSB).

# Chapter 7

## *Pack Up Your Lip Gloss*

*Strong women don't play victim, don't make themselves look pitiful, & don't point fingers. They stand and they deal.*

— Mandy Hale

When Kyle and I lost our business, I was at a career crossroads. I had been out of the computer industry for nine years, which was a lifetime in the world of computers. Many cops will tell you they always knew they were going to be cops. They either came from a family of first responders or wanted to be one ever since they were kids. That wasn't the case for me. I'd never really thought about it until this point in my life. What made me want to become a cop at the ripe old age of thirty-two, I'll never know. I do remember having a desire to help people and wanting to make a difference. I wanted something more than running my backside off for tips or writing computer code.

Not only was I eleven years older than most of the

people who began their law enforcement career, but I was also about forty pounds overweight, out of shape, and female. The hiring process was a rigorous series of phases that could take several weeks to complete. And you didn't just select a department you wanted to work for and call it good. The odds of being hired were steep, so to increase your chances, you had to apply and go through the hiring process with multiple police agencies. The goal was to be one of the top three candidates on the agency's hiring list. Once you made it on the list, it could take six months to a year before you were hired. The process was not for the faint of heart.

The first phase was a written exam. Now, back in 1989 -1990, there could be hundreds of people who would show up for a written exam when an agency was hiring for two or three positions. It depended on the agency. When I took the written exam for the city police department that hired me, four hundred people took the written exam, and the department was hiring two officers. The written exam consisted of questions involving math, English, and report writing. My score on the written exam was in the top ten percent, so I was moved to the second phase, which was the physical agility test. Now, I am far from the athletic type, and remember, I was out of shape and about forty pounds overweight. The physical agility test for all police agencies was the same test that was given to people who applied to the police academy, so I knew what to expect and had been "training" for it before I took the written exam.

In those days, the physical agility test consisted of a vertical jump, sit-ups, push-ups, and running 1.5 miles, each within an allotted period of time. When I started my training, I couldn't run five feet, couldn't do one push-up or sit-up, and could do a vertical jump of about three inches. No lie. I was a sad case physically. But I was determined, and after about three months of training, I dropped about fifteen pounds and was able to pass the physical agility test.

The next phase was a background check, which I passed with flying colors, and the phase after that was an interview in front of a panel of five high-ranking officers. Oh boy. Talk about being a bundle of nerves. I walked out of the interview not remembering a single question they asked or any of my responses, but I must have nailed it because I moved on to the final phase, the psychological evaluation.

The psychological evaluation consisted of a 1,000-question test in which the same group of questions was asked over and over again but phrased differently. It took three hours to complete the test. If you passed the psychological evaluation, you met with the police department's psychologist, who asked you questions like, "If you could be any animal, which animal would you be and why?" I guess I fit the psychological profile they were looking for, and they liked my police dog answer to the "If you could be any animal..." question as I made the shortlist. Now the waiting began.

It took a couple of weeks, but I finally got the call inviting me to meet with the Chief of Police of the department. That only meant one thing; if the Chief liked you, you were hired. The interview with the Chief was just a formality, but I could barely maintain my composure when he offered me the job. It had been a long process, and I had worked my backside off to get the job.

The next step was to graduate from the police academy with a Category II Law Enforcement Officer certification. A

Category II certification was required if you wanted to be a police officer, deputy sheriff, or highway patrol trooper. A Category I Special Functions Officer/Auxiliary Officer certification was a prerequisite to the Category II certification. A Category I certification allows you to be a constable, auxiliary officer, bailiff, reserve officer, and other special function officer. Category I training consists primarily of studying the criminal code, physical fitness training, and learning arrest control techniques. Category II training is when the fun begins, as it consists of classes like firearms training, accident investigation, crime scene scenarios, emergency vehicle operations, and arrest control techniques.

The police academy was three months of grueling, quasi-military training. We started each day in the gym doing push-ups and sit-ups and other calisthenics, which were followed by a 1.5-mile run outside, regardless of the weather. My three months in the academy were from October to December, so it wasn't unusual for us to return from a wintery run sopping wet and frozen to the core. We ran in the rain, sleet, snow, or shine. There was really no mercy given in any aspect of the academy. You either cut it, or you didn't. They didn't play favorites, and they didn't give anyone any special consideration. And, to top it off, the police department that hired me also paid for my police academy training, so if I didn't graduate, I would be out of a job. Hey, no pressure, right? No, none at all.

You had about twenty minutes to shower, get into uniform, and get your butt in the classroom after the morning physical training. My long hair lasted about three days before I cut it all off—no time for primping in the academy. If you were late to class, you would receive a demerit - too many demerits and you were out of there. I wasn't taking any chances.

The Category I block of the police academy was about ninety percent academics, which was fine by me. This was one of those times when my age and experience played in my favor. I'd had experience with academics, getting my bachelor's degree through an accelerated program of eighteen months and graduating with a 3.98 GPA. Many of the younger cadets had only graduated from high school and hadn't had to pump through a textbook every five weeks for eighteen months while working full-time and raising two children.

But, where the young cadets lacked in academic experience, they excelled in physical training. I, on the other hand, struggled. At the end of the police academy was a physical agility test that you had to pass in order to graduate. It was the same test I had trained for and taken when I applied to the police department, but the stakes were higher. The final test required running the 1.5 miles in less time, more sit-ups, more push-ups, and a higher vertical jump. I was petrified. When the others were studying for exams, I ran or did push-ups and sit-ups. If I failed the physical agility test, it wouldn't be for lack of trying.

The great thing about the academy, and law enforcement for that matter, is the camaraderie. Everyone at the academy helped and supported one another, whether that meant helping someone study for an exam or running alongside them after classes were done for the day. The stakes were high for all of us, but we were all in it together, and we all had each other's backs.

The police academy is definitely not a walk in the park. Recruits are tested on everything, and their success depends on passing all of the tests. They are not all easy tasks to complete, whether it be an exam on the criminal code or the final night time shoot when your fingers are frozen, but still expected to shoot an 85% to pass. My close call was on the Emergency Vehicle Operations (EVO) range. We'd been training for days for the final EVO test, which involved driving the course through an endless sea of orange traffic cones. Forward, backward, through twists and turns, parallel parking, sudden turns, and all in an allotted amount of time.

It was the final test day. We all stood on the border of the driving range, listening to the instructor give us final instructions. I was feeling pretty good about the whole thing until the instructor sternly said, "You know you have to pass this test in order to graduate from the police academy, so you better not screw up."

OH BOY! The minute the instructor said that I became paralyzed. Frozen with fear, I thought, "*What if I don't pass? If I don't pass, I will lose my job, and all of this hard work will have been for nothing. I can't afford to lose my job. OMG, I hope I can pull this off.*"

I climbed into the police vehicle assigned to me, which was a Crown Victoria, the worst vehicle I could be in to run the course. It was large, long, and clunky—the worst. My heart began to race, and my palms began to sweat as I crept forward in line. My turn. Here goes nothing. I didn't pass the first time through, or the second time, or the third through sixth times. I was ready to cry. I had one more chance to make it through the course in time and with minimal mistakes.

As I sat in the police cruiser waiting for my turn, one of my fellow cadets jumped into the passenger seat of the car.

"What are you doing?" I asked.

"I'm here to help you relax. You're too tense. You've got this," he replied and began to sing, "*Feelings, nothing more than feelings...*"

I busted out laughing and started the course. That cadet was with me through the entire course, helping me to relax, encouraging me, and building my confidence. When I drove over the finish line, we both let out a victory yelp as I received a thumbs up from the instructor, telling me I had passed the course! Camaraderie.

By the time I graduated from the police academy, I had lost another twenty pounds. I squeaked by the physical agility test and didn't graduate at the top of my class, but I did manage to earn a Pistol Marksman pin. Now it was show time. After graduating from the academy, I began my field training, which was three months long. I was assigned three Field Training Officers or FTOs, each of whom I would work with for one month. My first FTO was my primary FTO. He was the one with whom I would work the first month and the FTO who would critique my work the final week and have the final say as to whether or not I would be retained by the department. My second FTO was the officer who would teach me how to respond to traffic accidents and investigate them, and my third FTO would be the one who would polish as many rough edges as he could and prepare me for my final week.

The first shift of field training was kind of a freebie, as you rode shotgun in the police vehicle observing your FTO and learning the basics. You were under the spotlight on all subsequent shifts with your FTO watching your every move and listening to every word you said and how you said it. At the end of every shift, your FTO would grade you on that shift's performance by completing a Daily Observation Report or DOR. Every DOR was a mini-test you had to pass to graduate from field training. If you passed all of your DORs and the final week of field training, you would retain your job and could work solo. If not, you were out the door, and your career as a cop was over.

Field training was a repeat of the police academy in that the pressure was on, but different from the academy because now the scenarios were not happening in a controlled environment. It was real. There was no controlled combat, fake guns, or do-overs. Every day was a roll of the dice as to whether you would make it home alive or in one piece. Also, the police academy didn't and couldn't prepare you for what you would see and experience as a police officer.

I wasn't with my FTO for the first part of my first field training shift. My FTO was working on another assignment, so I shadowed one of the sergeants. Our first call was a suicide. A teenager had shot himself. When we arrived, several county sheriff's vehicles were parked in front of the residence. We entered the house through a side door and were immediately immersed in organized chaos. As we walked through the entry toward the kitchen, we made our way through several deputies who were gathered at the top of a staircase that led to the basement. As I passed the staircase, I looked down and saw a hand lying open on the floor next to what looked like the top of a head lying in a pool of blood. My stomach began to turn. The only dead person I had seen before this was Brandon. Flashbacks of Brandon lying bloody and mangled on the hospital bed began running through my brain.

"This is the county's jurisdiction, so we can leave." the sergeant said.

"What?" I asked, trying to come back to the present.

"This isn't our call because it's the county's jurisdiction, so we can leave," he repeated.

I stared down at the body lying lifeless at the bottom of the stairs.

"It was a sixteen-year-old boy. He shot himself with a shotgun. That's part of his brain lying there next to his head. Do you want to go down and look?"

My first thought was that I should be brave and go down those stairs, look at the crime scene, and learn as much as possible. But I chickened out and slowly shook my head. I couldn't bring myself to look at it. It was too soon. I wasn't prepared. It was then that I got a glimpse of what police work was about and began second-guessing my decision to become a police officer.

As we were walking back to the police vehicle, the sergeant, recognizing the look of hesitation and shock on my face, said sympathetically, "It's okay not to look. I couldn't look the first time I saw a dead body. You'll get used to it."

I wondered how it would be possible to "get used to it." And then I felt the intrigue and the guilt for feeling intrigued. On one hand, I was sickened, but on the other hand, I was curious about what exactly had happened and how it had happened. It was like a puzzle waiting to be solved - examining the crime scene, collecting evidence, and putting the pieces together to see the entire picture. I was hooked and knew then that my career goal would be to become a detective.

The first shift with my FTO started a little rocky as I made my first traffic stop. There's more to a traffic stop than meets the eye. Identifying a traffic violation sets in motion a series of steps that must be executed correctly and timed just right.

1. Identify the traffic violation and burn into your head the location of where the violation took place and what happened,
2. go into officer safety mode,
3. be prepared to run code if the driver doesn't stop and a chase ensues,
4. select a safe place where you will stop the vehicle,
5. turn on your red and blue flashing lights,
6. get on the radio and let dispatch know you're making a traffic stop and tell them the location where the stop will take place, as well as the license number, vehicle type, and color of the vehicle,
7. park behind the vehicle as you were taught at the police academy,
8. approach the vehicle as you were taught at the police academy,
9. speak with the driver and ask for their driver's license, registration, and proof of insurance,
10. go back to your car and ask dispatch to run the driver's license and registration,
11. get the information from dispatch,

12. write a ticket and/or make an arrest.

During field training, all this is done with your FTO sitting in the passenger seat, watching every move you make. There is no room for error. I don't remember why I stopped the vehicle, but I was nervous. It was not only my first ever real live traffic stop, it was the first time I talked to dispatch on the radio. I managed to make the stop with no hiccups, but as I opened the car door to exit the vehicle, I heard my FTO calmly say, "You might want to put the car in park." It wasn't until then that I realized the car was slowly creeping forward. It's funny now, but it definitely was not funny at the time. I thought my FTO would have logged the incident in my DOR, but for some reason, he let it slide, and for that, I will be eternally grateful.

I became a cop in 1990. At that time, female police officers weren't scarce, but they certainly weren't the majority. Another female officer was hired shortly before I was. Together, we drove the percentage of female officers in the department up to a whopping eight percent. The percentage of female police officers hasn't changed much in the last thirty-two years. In 2022, women made up just 12% of the law enforcement officers in the country and 3% of police leadership[1].

Most of the male officers made us feel welcome, but some members of the "good old boys" club at the department thought women had no business being police officers. My first encounter with one of the good old boys was during the first month of my field training. I was working an afternoon shift and went to the briefing room to write a report. Sitting off to the side in an interview room was an older male officer named Bradshaw, who was also writing a report. I was familiar with Bradshaw but hadn't really talked with him much. I took a seat and began writing.

After a few minutes, Bradshaw laid down his pen, and out of nowhere, he sternly said, "You're not going to make it through field training."

In other words, *You're a woman, and women can't cut it as cops, so pack up your lip gloss and get the hell out of here.* I immediately knew it was a make-it-or-break-it moment. My response would either earn his respect or taint his opinion of me forever.

I chose respect.

"You know what. F— you, Bradshaw." I responded with the most flippant attitude I could muster. Bradshaw grinned, took a drink of his coffee, and went back to writing his report.

Kyle and I divorced shortly after I graduated from field training. I was a single mom beginning a new career and had no idea how I would make it all work. Back then, the beginning wage for a police officer at the police department where I worked was $18,500 per year. You certainly didn't become a cop for the money. I managed to make ends meet by working multiple part-time jobs in addition to my full-time job as a police officer. My part-time jobs were usually security jobs at the mall or the local skating rink or picking up some overtime traffic shifts.

Because I was a rookie, I worked the day shift. Shift bidding took place every three months, and those who had seniority could get the coveted afternoon shift, which was the busiest and most exciting shift. The graveyard shift filled up next, and those with the least seniority or those working as resource officers at a grade school ended up with the day shift. Day shift was the least exciting shift, as the predominant calls during the day shift were juvenile problems, traffic accidents, and property crimes that had taken place the night before. But I wasn't complaining. Working day shift allowed me to work while my kids were in school.

This divorce was the worst one yet. Not because Kyle and I screamed and yelled at each other but because of the girls. At that age, they couldn't really understand what was going on. But the alternative was worse. Kyle and I fighting every day would not have been good for their psyche. But still, leaving Kyle was very hard for me to do. After nine years of marriage, I still loved him, and part of me was very sad that such a good marriage had come crumbling down around us, all because of a dream.

## Reflection of Hope

We all encounter crossroads in our lifetime, and sometimes we look back and think, *How would my life be now if I had taken road A instead of road B? Did I make the right decision? Would I be making more money? Would my marriage have lasted? Would I be happier?* These are questions that are impossible to know the answers to, and going down the what-if road will make you crazy. Would I have made more money as a computer programmer? Probably. I certainly wouldn't have married Kyle and had my two daughters. Would my marriage have lasted had I married someone else? Maybe. Maybe not.

We need to look back at what we've done instead of wondering what could have been. If I'd taken a different career path, I wouldn't have been able to help all the people I did during my twenty years as an officer. I may have had children, but I wouldn't have my daughters and the grandchildren that I love so dearly. We make choices with the information and experience we have at the time. Are they always the right choices? No, they're not.

Life is hard and wonderful all at the same time. One Sunday in church, our pastor passed the microphone to the congregation and asked us to tell everyone what they were thankful for. One of the members said he was thankful for what God had taken away from him because if God had allowed him to have these things, it would have been to his detriment, and it wouldn't have been pretty. He also said he was thankful that his life wasn't easy because there is pain in producing good things.

There certainly was pain in having two children, in training for the police academy, in completing field training, in losing weight, in getting a bachelor's degree, in so many things I've done in my life, but my fellow church member was absolutely right. There is pain in producing the good things we choose to produce. What is tricky and sometimes very difficult is to find the good things in the pain we don't choose to produce—finding the silver lining.

What was the silver lining in having an abortion against my will? Maybe it made the decision to have my first daughter easier to make. Perhaps it made me stronger. Maybe it gave me the empathy I needed to volunteer at a pregnancy resource center and have the opportunity to dissuade pregnant girls and women from having an abortion. Silver linings are what you and you alone can find, as they are unique and personal to only you. And, it is crucial that we look for them.

What do we do when we absolutely cannot find a silver lining in the pain? We pray and know that we can find peace in the Lord. In Romans 5:3-4 (NLT), Paul says in his letter to the Roman church, *We can rejoice, too, when we run into problems and trials, for we know that they help us develop endurance. And endurance develops strength of character, and character strengthens our confident hope of salvation.*

There is great wisdom and promise in these words. Paul said problems and trials help us develop endurance, and endurance develops strength of character. Our experiences and our pain have made us stronger and have given us the ability to handle pain much better this time than we did the last time or avoid it altogether. But what is the end game here? The end game is salvation and being with God when we leave this place. All of this pain and heartache is temporary. There will be an end to it. Paul said, "...character strengthens our confident hope of salvation. And this hope will not lead to disappointment. For we know how dearly God loves us because he has given us the Holy Spirit to fill our hearts with his love," (Romans 5:5 NLT). By building our spiritual character, we will put our faith and hope in God and the salvation given to us through Christ's death and resurrection, and we will know this earthly pain is temporary for those who believe in Him.

## Scriptures of Hope

✝ My flesh and my heart faileth: but God is the strength of my heart, and my portion forever. (Psalm 73:26 KJV)

✝ I can do all things through Christ who strengthens me. (Philippians 4:13 NKJV).

✝ But as for me, I will sing about your power. Each morning I will sing with joy about your unfailing love. For you have been my refuge, a place of safety when I am in distress. (Psalm 59:16 NLT)

✝ I have told you these things, so that in me you may have peace. In this world you will have trouble. But take heart! I have overcome the world. (John 16:33 NIV).

✝ Fear not, for I am with you; be not dismayed, for I am your God; I will strengthen you, I will help you, I will uphold you with my righteous right hand. (Isaiah 41:10 ESV).

✝ This is my command—be strong and courageous! Do not be afraid or discouraged. For the LORD your God is with you wherever you go. (Joshua 1:9 NLT).

✝ And after you have suffered a little while, the God of all grace, who has called you to his eternal glory in Christ, will himself restore, establish, and strengthen you. (1 Peter 5:10 RSV).

✝ But they that wait upon the LORD shall renew their strength; they shall mount up with wings as eagles; they shall run, and not be weary; and they shall walk, and not faint. (Isaiah 40:31 KJV).

✝ Give all your worries and cares to God, for he cares about you. (1 Peter 5:7 NLT).

✝ Yea, though I walk through the valley of the shadow of death, I will fear no evil; For You are with me; Your rod and Your staff, they comfort me. (Psalm 23:4 NKJV).

# Chapter 8

## *Every Time They Put On The Uniform*

*All gave some. Some gave all.*

— Howard William Osterkamp

I met my fourth husband, Ryan, about six months after my divorce from Kyle. Ryan was a detective at the police department, and I was working patrol. Ryan was confident and charismatic and held the position at the police department that I coveted the most. Any position other than a patrol officer was considered a specialty, and you had to work patrol for three years before applying for a specialty position. I was counting down the days.

When I met Ryan, I was again searching for love. I was still trying to find my wholeness through a relationship – still desperately searching. I loved Ryan deeply. Not as deeply as I loved Alex, but close. We were on again, off again, for three years before we got married, and that's when things changed.

What I thought was a trusting, loving relationship turned out to be yet another betrayal.

About one week after we got married, Ryan told me he wasn't attracted to me anymore. When I asked him why, he said it was because I was a police officer. This obviously came as a shock to me, as he'd known me as nothing else but a cop. He then told me he wanted me to quit the police department.

"Stop being a police officer? What do you want me to do, scoop ice cream at Baskin Robbins?" I asked.

"Yes," he replied.

I was astounded and couldn't believe what I was hearing. *He met me when I was a cop. I've been a cop the entire time we have been together. I thought he loved me. What is happening?*

I thought it was unfair of him to ask me to stop being a cop, and I wasn't about to do so. That was the first wrinkle in our very short marriage. The second wrinkle was the neighbor lady.

During one of our break-ups, Ryan slept with the neighbor who lived at the end of the street. It didn't surprise me, as I'd seen them openly flirting with each other while Ryan and I were visiting her at her house one day. To me, it was obvious, but I didn't say anything to Ryan about it for fear I was overreacting and the truth was they had been neighbors for a long time and were just good friends. When I later asked Ryan about their relationship, he was very honest and told me he slept with her during one of our break-ups. He saw my reaction to this news. The neighbor was now off-limits. I thought that was reasonable. But I guess Ryan didn't have the same point of view.

Ryan wasn't kidding when he said he wasn't attracted to me anymore, as a couple of weeks later, he hooked up with the neighbor again. When I found out, I packed up everything I had moved into his house, took my girls, and left him. Cheating is not something I can tolerate. I'm not the type of person who can work through something like that. Some women are. I'm not. Once the trust has been broken on such a monumental scale, I don't have it in me to trust again. As far as I was concerned, it was over.

This divorce was probably the hardest one for me. Worse than the divorce with Kyle. I loved Ryan very much and couldn't get over him. I spent the next year sobbing over the loss, wishing we could be together again and wondering if the pain would ever subside. It's the hoping and wishing that keeps your heart in chains. *Maybe I could forgive him? I can never forgive the betrayal. Maybe I can look past the betrayal and trust him again. I don't know how I will ever be able to forgive and forget. Maybe there is hope for us? There is no hope for us.* I didn't want to give up hope. As long as I had hope, the possibility of us being together was kept alive. At least in my mind. It was the realization that there was no hope for us that allowed me to dry my tears and leave Ryan behind.

A position became available in the detective division working property crimes. I had put in my three years in patrol, so when the position became available, I jumped at the chance and submitted my application. Now, property crimes are not what I wanted to investigate. I wanted to investigate person crimes. Property crimes included crimes like bad checks, theft, and credit card fraud. I wanted to investigate crimes like rape, assault, child abuse, and homicide. But it was a way to get my foot in the door of the detective division, which is exactly what happened. Six months after working property crimes, I was transferred to person crimes. I thought I had died and gone to heaven. My dream had finally become a reality.

After working in the detective division for about a year, an opportunity came along to teach criminal justice classes at the community college as an adjunct professor. I had been helping with domestic violence classes at the police academy and found I really loved teaching. So, when this opportunity came along, I grabbed it. I was part of the criminal justice department at the college and taught introduction to criminal justice and criminal investigation classes. After about a year of teaching at the community college, I began also teaching domestic violence and child abuse classes at the police academy. Teaching became my second job, allowing me to quit my part-time security jobs.

I had become somewhat of an expert at investigating child abuse cases. I attended every child abuse training course that came along, and most of my caseload consisted of child abuse cases. Emotionally, these were the hardest cases to investigate and the most challenging. They are also the cases you will carry with you long after you turn in your badge. I had one such case shortly after I was transferred to the person crimes division.

A woman who looked after the children during the service at her church called concerning the behavior of a five-year-old girl she had tended to at church the previous Sunday. Church service had ended, and the mother's boyfriend had come to pick up the girl from the childcare area. The woman was concerned because when he came to pick up the girl, she didn't want to go with him. Not because she was having fun or didn't want to leave her playmates, but because she seemed afraid of him.

This was the first child abuse case I had been assigned, and I had no clue what to do. Thankfully, one of the senior investigators offered to go to the girl's house with me to check on her and interview the girl's mother and her boyfriend. Luckily, when we went to the house, all three of them were home. Interviews of the mother and her boyfriend didn't raise any red flags to either of us.

The mother allowed me to take her daughter into another room and check for bruises, bumps, or any other suspicious-looking marks on her daughter's body. The two small bruises I did find were on her shins, which didn't seem abnormal, as all the while we were there the girl was extremely active, running all over the place and bumping into furniture and toys. The senior investigator and I discussed what we had found and neither one of us thought there was cause to call Child Protective Services, so we left and closed the case.

About a month later when I went to work, the senior investigator approached me and said, "Do you remember that case where we went to the five-year-old girl's house and interviewed the girl's mother and her boyfriend?"

"Yes," I replied, wondering why he was asking.

"She's dead," he said.

My mouth dropped open with shock, and I burst into uncontrollable tears. I couldn't believe what I was hearing.

*What did we miss? She seemed fine. The responses to the interview questions were appropriate and seemed sincere. Where did I go wrong? Is it my fault this poor girl is dead?*

*What am I doing here? I have no business investigating child abuse cases. But, I checked the girl for inappropriate marks on her body. We checked the house. We interviewed the mother and the boyfriend. What the hell happened?*

My lieutenant called me into his office. "I'm taking you off this case," he said.

"No, please don't. I can handle it," I said, sniffling with tears running down my face.

"No, I think it's best if you didn't work this case. I'm going to reassign it to another investigator."

He was right to do so. I was a mess and wasn't thinking clearly. This case was likely a homicide and someone who wasn't so emotionally involved should investigate the case.

The investigator who took over the case was sympathetic and kept me in the loop every step of the way, which I greatly appreciated. As it turned out, the case was a homicide. The mother had gone out for the evening and left her daughter with her boyfriend. The girl didn't want to eat, so the boyfriend lost it, picked her up, and banged her head against the wall hard enough to cause a subdural hematoma on the back of her head and retinal hemorrhages, which is usually a sign of shaken baby.

When the mother came home, she found her daughter lying on the floor of the entrance to the split-level home. The boyfriend told her not to call an ambulance and insisted on taking the girl to the hospital himself. At the hospital, the boyfriend told a police officer the girl was walking along the railing and fell to the floor but told the mother the girl had fallen over the back of the couch, which was sitting alongside the railing.

The mother, who was pregnant with her boyfriend's

baby, believed her boyfriend and stuck by his side throughout the investigation and court process. It wasn't until the trial that the boyfriend wrote a confession and gave it to the judge in a sealed envelope. He was convicted and sentenced to five years in prison. This case is one I will never forget. I've come to terms with it and truly believe there was nothing I could have done at the time. But it still haunts me. I still feel guilt. I still feel the pain. I suspect I always will.

I spent the next seventeen years investigating a myriad of different types of cases, including rape, child sexual and physical abuse, homicide, securities fraud, computer crime, white-collar crime, fraud, and elder abuse and exploitation. Most people go through their lives oblivious to the ugliness and evil that exists in the world. They've never witnessed tragedy.

They've never seen the mother of a fourteen-year-old boy frantically attempting to remove the rope from around her dead son's neck as he hangs from the clothing rod in his closet. They've never seen a sixteen-year-old boy sitting in the driver's seat of his truck that he parked next to a park before he blew his head off with a shotgun. They've never seen the battered or burned bodies of children who have been physically abused or a child who is self-mutilating in an attempt to manage the emotions created by the sexual abuse they have experienced.

These are a fraction of examples of what law enforcement officers see every time they put on the uniform to go to work. It's no wonder that law enforcement officers have a 54% increase in suicide risk when compared to the civilian population[1]. Every time they check on for work, police officers are likely to encounter tragedy or fight to prevent it. They put their lives and their mental health on the line every time they put on the uniform, and they do it to protect others and make a difference in this world.

It was common for people to ask me if I'd ever shot anyone or if I'd ever been shot while on the job. I was one of the lucky ones who never had to shoot anyone and who had never been shot. I had suffered injuries while on the job, but my injuries were unseen. But you know, I wouldn't change one day of my twenty years as a police officer. I know I made a difference in some people's lives, and I am grateful for that. I once had a citizen ask me if I was afraid I might die while on duty. I told her I wasn't, because I couldn't think of a more noble way to die.

## Reflection of Hope

I feel like I have felt enough heartbreak and pain and seen enough tragedy for ten lifetimes.

This reflection will be the hardest for me to write, as I never talked about any of my police experiences in therapy, so they still haunt me. Yeah, I know. I need to go back to therapy and deal with it. I don't really ever think about them much, so writing about some of them now kind of brings it home. But, this is the Reflection of Hope, so I'll try not to be too dismal and find the silver lining somewhere among the wreckage.

I remember a number of the tragic cases I investigated, and as I think about them, the original pain or profound sadness is felt as if it were yesterday. What was my role in all of it? Well, I signed up to help people and make a difference in my community. How did I help the mother who was trying to free her son from the noose by not allowing her to do so? I couldn't tell her about evidence collection and preserving the scene. It may be a homicide, and to remove the noose from someone who was obviously dead would ruin the crime scene, which would wipe out the evidence needed to solve the case. But, I couldn't tell her something like that while she was frantic and desperate and in so much pain.

For a moment, I was living the experience with the boy's mother. I saw the mother's pain and allowed it to seep into my skin. The picture of the boy hanging by a rope in his closet will forever be burned in my mind as I'm sure it is in his mother's. The only thing I could do was to softly tell her he was gone, gently lead her out of the room, and put my arm around her as she sobbed.

So what is the silver lining? The silver lining is all of the people I was able to help. When I think of them, it makes me smile and lightens the load. And, I'm sure I made a difference in some people's lives of which I am completely unaware, which I'm sure we all do. Only when I look at my law enforcement career as a whole can I say it was worth it and I would do it all again in a heartbeat.

I also find great comfort in knowing that this life of mine is but a flicker in the grand scheme of things. I am a spirit inside of a body so that I can accomplish what I need to on this earth. I find peace and solace in knowing my human life is but a nanosecond of my everlasting spiritual existence. That when I leave this place, I will be with Jesus and will know the glory of God.

## Scriptures of Hope

✝ And God shall wipe away all tears from their eyes; and there shall be no more death, neither sorrow, nor crying, neither shall there be any more pain: for the former things are passed away. (Revelation 21:4 KJV).

✝ For God so loved the world that He gave His only begotten Son, that whoever believes in
Him should not perish but have everlasting life. (John 3:16 NKJV).

✝ Don't store up treasures here on earth, where moths eat them and rust destroys them, and where thieves break in and steal. Store your treasures in heaven, where moths and rust cannot destroy, and thieves do not break in and steal. (Matthew 6:19-20 NLT).

✝ Since, then, you have been raised with Christ, set your hearts on things above, where Christ is, seated at the right hand of God. Set your minds on things above, not on earthly things. (Colossians 3:2 NIV).

✝ I am the living bread that came down from heaven. If anyone eats of this bread, he will live forever. And the bread that I will give for the life of the world is my flesh. (John 6:51 ESV).

✝ For we do not have an enduring city here; instead, we seek the one to come. (Hebrews 13:14 CSB).

✝ For our citizenship is in heaven, from which also we eagerly wait for a Savior, the Lord Jesus Christ, who will transform the body of our humble state into conformity with the body of His glory, by His working through which He is able to even subject all things to Himself. (Philippians 3:20-21 LSB).

✝ Beloved, now are we the sons of God, and it doth not yet appear what we shall be: but we know that, when he shall appear, we shall be like him; for we shall see him as he is. (1 John 3:2 KJV).

✝ I say to you that likewise there will be more joy in heaven over one sinner who repents than over ninety-nine just persons who need no repentance. (Luke 15:7 NKJV).

✝ Yes, and the Lord will deliver me from every evil attack and will bring me safely into his heavenly Kingdom. All glory to God forever and ever! Amen. (2 Timothy 4:18 NLT).

# Chapter 9

## *The Polygamist Husband*

*And he shall not acquire many wives for himself, lest his heart turn away, nor shall he acquire for himself excessive silver and gold.*

— Deuteronomy 17:17 ESV

My fifth husband, Dennis, was a former polygamist. He was from Canada and came to the United States to join a polygamist group. He was a self-taught master craftsman and earned a living by working odd jobs and remodeling homes. At the time, I was still rejecting God and wasn't an active churchgoer. Neither was Dennis, although he was well-versed in the scriptures and other religious books. Dennis had been expelled from a polygamist group for several years when I met him and had given up that way of life, or so I thought.

Dennis had only one wife when he was part of the polygamist group. Not that he didn't want more wives, he did, but he was banned from the group before he could take another wife. Dennis's polygamist wife had four children when they married, and they had three children together. Dennis's wife didn't work outside the home and Dennis earned a meager living working within the confines of the group. He once told me he and his family would look for food in dumpsters that were behind grocery stores and how excited they were one night when they found a box full of discarded yogurt.

Dennis and his wife were very committed to the group, and over time, Dennis developed a close relationship with one of the group leaders. Aspiring to become a group leader, Dennis immersed himself in religious study and considered himself a prophet. When Dennis proclaimed his epiphany to the group leaders, they wasted no time banning him from the group.

Before we married, Dennis assured me he had left the polygamist way of life behind and no longer wanted multiple wives. I would never tolerate this, and I made that very clear to him. But after our first year of marriage, Dennis began to change slowly. The change in Dennis started when his twelve-year-old son showed up at our house out of the blue. It was a cold and snowy winter night when we heard the doorbell ring and found John standing outside the door dressed in tennis shoes, long pants, and a long-sleeved shirt. He had no coat on, was soaking wet, and was shivering. John fled from the polygamist community, riding his bicycle in the snow for hours in hopes that he would find his dad and find refuge from the group.

John had lived a very sheltered life in the polygamist community. This became very apparent as I learned things about him, like he had never been to a movie theater, to school, or shopping, or had never eaten a piece of pie. When I took him to a shoe store to get him a new pair of shoes, he was astounded that there was a store that sold nothing but shoes. He'd never been to a store before and was mesmerized as we wandered through the aisles.

"Here are the shoes in your size. Pick out a pair that you like," I said.

John looked at me befuddled.

Realizing John had never had a new pair of shoes, much less had been given a choice as to which pair of shoes he could have, I showed him all of the shoes that were his size and told him to select a pair that he liked and try them on to see how they fit. John looked at the shelves full of shoes and pointed to a pair of tennis shoes he wanted to try. I took them off the shelf and laid them on the floor in front of him.

"Go ahead and try them on," I said.

John looked at the shoes and then looked at me apprehensively. Sensing his anxiety, I placed my hand on his shoulder and said, "It's okay. Everyone tries on shoes before they buy them to see if they fit and are comfortable."

John tried on the shoes, carefully lacing them, and then sat there looking at them on his feet.

"Walk around in them to see how they feel," I instructed.

John stood up and walked up and down the aisle, staring at the shoes with every step.

"How do they feel?" I asked.

"They feel good," John said timidly.

"Are those the shoes you want, or do you want to try on another pair?" I asked.

"I like these," John said.

"Okay, put your shoes back on and let's go up front and pay for these."

John intently watched every step of the shoe-buying transaction and then smiled as I handed him the bag containing his first pair of new shoes.

Watching John experience the things in life that we take for granted and consider part of our routine was humbling. The first time we took John to a restaurant was much like the shoe-buying experience in that he felt like he was in a foreign land and had no idea what to do. He had never been to a place where you sat in a room full of strangers, looked at a list of food options, ordered whatever you wanted, and had someone serve you your food. But once he got the hang of it, watching John try new foods, especially desserts, was truly like watching a kid in a candy store.

John was extremely bright and adapted to his new life fairly quickly. Going to public school was a challenge for him at first because the public school system would only allow him to start school in the grade that was age-appropriate. John had been homeschooled, but not to the grade level he needed to be for public school. But, despite his academic handicap, it didn't take long before John excelled in his studies. It was the social aspect of public school that gave John the most trouble. John had never been in an environment where there were so many teenagers with whom he was unfamiliar. Making friends was nearly impossible for John, as he was fairly introverted and had a background that he wasn't eager to share for fear he would be ridiculed.

As Dennis changed, I began to see a side of him I hadn't seen before, a side that was very foreign to me. He became distant and began spending more and more time studying religious writings, particularly of the Mormon religion. It was as if having John living under the same roof gave him a longing for the polygamist life he had left behind. This became apparent to me when we took the girls and John to a buffet for dinner one night. As we finished our meal, Dennis stared at the family sitting at the table beside us. There was nothing strange about them, but for some reason, Dennis was watching them very closely.

It wasn't until the family left the restaurant that I realized Dennis had been formulating a plan, as he immediately got up and went and sat at their table and began eating the food they had left behind. I couldn't believe what I was seeing.

"What are you doing?" I asked him.

Dennis shrugged his shoulders and said, "They left. I'm not going to let it go to waste."

I was in shock and looked around to see if anyone else was staring at him. Luckily, no one seemed to have noticed. I was so embarrassed and indiscreetly motioned to Dennis to return to our table. He did so unwillingly, but not before he grabbed a couple of pieces of pizza and brought them to our table.

I could see Dennis slowly settling into his old ways, but it wasn't until Dennis and I took John to his mother's house to visit his brothers and sisters that he drastically changed. It had been about a year since John had left the polygamist community. His mother was now the third wife of a polygamist man in the group and had given birth to three of his children. It was a cool fall day, and as we parked the car in front of the weathered Victorian-style home, I could see the faces of children peering out of almost every window. A small boy wearing only a diaper ran across the front lawn as a young teenage girl emerged through the front door and quickly ran after him.

The remaining siblings came pouring out of the house to greet their long-lost brother. John was grinning from ear to ear, soaking in all of the heartwarming attention. As I watched John's brothers and sisters greet him, I wondered how it must feel to have a family so eager to see you, and that loved and missed you so much. We walked into the house and onto the worn, bare wooden living room floors. A strong, cool breeze came through a broken-out window, making the torn curtains flutter around a rocking chair sitting in the corner. The living room looked bare, as the rocking chair was the only piece furnishing the large room.

John's mother greeted him from the doorway of the adjacent kitchen. John clearly was more excited to see his siblings than he was his mother but gave her the warmest greeting he could muster. John's mother seemed agitated as she watched the older children rummage through the sparse kitchen cabinets, looking for something to eat and to feed the younger children. I watched as they opened each cabinet, hoping food would magically appear, each time with greater disappointment. Finally, the oldest daughter happened upon some dried food-storage food. Her face lit up, and she hollered as if she had won the lottery. John's mother seemed embarrassed that we had witnessed their poverty and immediately grabbed the food from her daughter's hand and began its preparation.

"My family is going to church. May I go with them?" John asked.

Dennis and I were hesitant but told John he could go if we accompanied him to the service. The last church I had been in was the Lutheran church my family and I attended when I was a child. When John asked if he could go to church with his family, this image immediately came to mind, leaving me ill-prepared for what was to come.

As we approached the church, I noticed the many children running around and playing and the strong sense of community among the people. It was like nothing I had ever seen, and I looked forward to the warm greeting I anticipated we would receive. But, as we walked through the doors of the church, there were no smiles or handshakes waiting for us. No welcoming faces. Only icy stares and a strong sense of contempt for the strangers who dared to walk into what they thought was an impenetrable domain.

As we hesitantly took our seats in one of the pews, the people sitting in the pew immediately slid away from us with scornful looks on their faces, making a great space between us as if we were lepers. The service began with a hymn, and then a regiment of rituals and testimonies began. The service concluded with the church leader preaching a fire and brimstone sermon designed to keep the community in check and maintain his authority over them. As we left, John mingled with some of the children and Dennis attempted to greet a few familiar faces but was immediately shunned by them. It was apparent that he wasn't welcome and they wanted nothing to do with him.

After our visit, Dennis began working less and became completely immersed in his religious study. It was as if spending time in the polygamist environment had catapulted him back in time and he was desperate to recreate it. Dennis would spend all day studying, and when I came home from work, he would commence with a dissertation on subjects like the Adam-God Theory. It got to the point where Dennis was so absorbed in the Mormon religion that he came to declare himself a prophet and told me he wanted to take another wife and live the polygamist lifestyle again. Wow! I couldn't believe my ears and never expected this to happen. Of course I didn't agree to Dennis' proposal and had no choice but to divorce him.

It took quite a while before I recovered from the shock of it all. I blamed myself for not seeing it coming. I believed Dennis when he told me he had left the polygamist life behind, but I couldn't help but think that I should have known there was a chance he was lying to himself. I guess I was lying to myself. This is yet another example of my wanting love so badly that I ignored what should have been the obvious.

## Reflection of Hope

Ignoring the obvious in order to have love was the story of my life. Wanting love is such a driving force. Rather, I should say, *needing* love is such a driving force. I was so desperate to have someone who loved me that I was willing to overlook the glaring possibility that Dennis hadn't truly left the polygamist lifestyle behind. I took his assurance that he had left it behind at face value because that's what I wanted to believe. That's what I did. I believed whatever I needed to so that I wouldn't have to face my fear of being alone.

In his autobiography entitled *Will,* actor Will Smith talks about making decisions based on fear. He said, "The fears create desires, and the desires precipitate actions. These repetitive actions and predictable responses are the building blocks of great cinematic characters. It's pretty much the same in real life. Something bad happens to us, and we decide we'll never let that happen again. But in order to prevent it, we have to be a certain way. We choose the behaviors that we believe will deliver safety, stability, and love. And we repeat them over and over again. In the movies, we call it a character. In real life, we call it personality. How we decide to respond to our fears, that is the person we become." I definitely chose the behaviors that I thought would "...deliver safety, stability and love." But, at times, it was all pretense. When it came to love, I became very adept at knowing who I needed to be. But, the sad thing is, I believed I was the person I was pretending to be.

By coming home, I have found true safety, stability, and love in the Lord Jesus Christ. The funny and strange thing is, I receive these things simply by being my true self. Jesus loves me and provides spiritual safety to me despite my flaws and fears. He loves me for who I truly am. He loves ME. I don't have to pretend to be someone I'm not to gain his favor. I don't have to say all the right things to have His love. I simply accept him as my Savior and know that he sacrificed himself for me. There is no greater love than His.

## Scriptures of Hope

✝ For since our friendship with God was restored by the death of his Son while we were still his enemies, we will certainly be saved through the life of his Son. (Romans 5:10 NLT).

✝ And so we know and rely on the love God has for us. God is love. Whoever lives in love lives in God, and God in them. (1 John 4:16 NIV).

✝ Yet in all these things we are more than conquerors through Him who loved us. For I am persuaded that neither death nor life, nor angels nor principalities nor powers, nor things present nor things to come, nor height nor depth, nor any other created thing, shall be able to separate us from the love of God which is in Christ Jesus our Lord. (Romans 8:37-39 NKJV).

✝ Behold, what manner of love the Father hath bestowed upon us, that we should be called the sons of God: therefore the world knoweth us not, because it knew him not. (1 John 3:1 KJV).

✝ But God, who is rich in mercy, because of his great love that he had for us, made us alive with Christ even though we were dead in trespasses. You are saved by grace! (Ephesians 2:4-5 CSB).

✝ We love, because He first loved us. (1 John 4:19 LSB).

✝ There is no fear in love; but perfect love casteth out fear: because fear hath torment. He that feareth is not made perfect in love. (1 John 4:18 KJV).

✝ My old self has been crucified with Christ. It is no longer I who live, but Christ lives in me. So I live in this earthly body by trusting in the Son of God, who loved me and gave himself for me. (Galatians 2:20 NLT).

✝ "For the mountains may depart and the hills be removed, but my steadfast love shall not depart from you, and my covenant of peace shall not be removed," says the Lord, who has compassion on you. ( Isaiah 54:10 ESV).

✝ Give thanks to the God of heaven! His faithful love endures forever. (Psalm 136:26 CSB).

# Chapter 10

## *Three Strikes. I'm out*

*If you spend your time hoping someone will suffer the consequences for what they did to your heart, then you're allowing them to hurt you a second time in your mind.*

— Shannon L. Adler

I met my sixth husband, Jason, on an online dating site. You'd think I would have been done with relationships after my marriage to Dennis, but nope, not even after an ex-polygamist husband did I give up on my endeavor to find love. Jason had a stable job, was a family man, and made me feel special. The made-me-feel-special part clinched it for me and made me overlook Jason's love of whiskey.

Jason had two children from a previous marriage, one of whom lived with us. By this time, my youngest daughter was living with me, and my oldest daughter was living with her dad. One of the things that attracted me to Jason was that he was a family man. Blending families is not easy, but Jason and I were committed to our children and a sense of family, so blending our two families came easily.

It was a couple of years into the marriage when Jason's love of videography and his discontent with his job made him want to pursue a business creating training videos for the maintenance industry. I agreed to help him by writing the scripts, screening actors, and directing the films. Jason's job was to shoot the videos, edit them, and turn them into the final product. We made a pretty good team, but life became hectic as Jason and I worked full-time jobs and raised our family while trying to get the training video business off the ground.

We had been working at the training video business for about a year when I learned that I had contracted hepatitis C. I applied for a police officer position at a city police department and was about to be hired, but first, I had to pass a physical exam. It was when I was in the Captain's office thinking I was there to be offered a position that the Captain told me I had hepatitis C. I was in shock.

*How in the world did I contract hepatitis C? How long have I had this? What do I do now?*

I knew hepatitis C was contracted through a transfer of blood from an infected individual to one who was not infected and that a common way of contracting it was through needle sharing.

I began to mentally review my entire police career in an effort to pinpoint a call that I'd been on where I may have made contact with infected blood. It wasn't until I played back to a time when I was searching under the front seat of a vehicle for illegal drugs. Like an idiot, I hadn't put my leather gloves on before reaching under the seat and paid for my stupid move by getting stuck in the finger with a used needle. Now, I can't be certain it was the needle stick from where I became infected. It could just as easily have been from unexpectedly engaging in a fight with a drug user. This is something I will never be certain of.

I immediately sought out a gastroenterologist who could treat my condition. The first thing they needed to do was a biopsy of my liver to determine the best treatment options. After the results of the biopsy came back, my doctor set me up on a six-month chemotherapy regimen of oral medication and interferon shots that I would give myself every day for the next six months. If I could make it through the next six months of chemotherapy, there was a very good chance the hepatitis C would be eradicated. I've never felt so sick as I did during chemotherapy. And this wasn't a feel-lousy-for-a-couple-of-hours-after-the-shot kind of sick. This was a feel-almost-like-you-want-to-die-all-the-time kind of sick. The closest I can come to describing it is to feel as though you have an extreme case of both the flu and pneumonia with a good dose of nausea all at the same time.

I made it through only three months of chemotherapy. I felt so horrible all the time; I just couldn't do it anymore. I could work only part-time and did nothing but lay in bed feeling sick when I wasn't working. I decided I would rather take my chances with what was left of the hepatitis C than feel like I was feeling twenty-four-seven-three-sixty-five. I made an appointment with my gastroenterologist to tell him I was done. I explained to him that I was so sick I couldn't function and I wasn't going to continue the chemotherapy. That's when he told me that for the last three months, I was receiving a double dose of the medication, so he was fine with me discontinuing the treatment. *What? I didn't know I was receiving a double dose of that stuff. Why didn't you tell me?* I didn't know whether to be mad or grateful. I decided to be grateful when I took a hepatitis C test, and it came back negative. It was completely worth it. I was hep C free.

What was almost as bad as going through chemotherapy was the absence of Jason, all the while I was sick. He was so obsessed with the video business that I only saw him when he went to bed. Not once did he come up to the bedroom to ask me how I was doing or to see if I needed anything. But that wasn't the worst of it. When a potential buyer came in from out-of-town and voiced his interest in the training videos, despite me being sick as a dog, Jason insisted I begin to write the script for a new video they had discussed. I was beside myself and couldn't believe he could be that cold-hearted. That was strike one.

Strike two was when Jason started drinking more heavily. I'm not sure exactly why he did. It may have been his discontent with his job or the fact that the video business was such a failure that we ended up filing personal bankruptcy. It got to the point where Jason was drinking nearly every day, and not just a few drinks. Toward the end of our marriage, Jason would start drinking after he came home from work, and by the time I got home, he would have polished off half a bottle of whiskey. I had overlooked Jason's drinking in the beginning, but it was getting out of hand. I started wondering if I had made a mistake marrying Jason.

Of course, life changed after we filed bankruptcy. We had to go into frugal mode, and if we wanted to purchase a big-ticket item, we had to save for it before we could buy it. You know, like my parents' generation did. It was an adjustment, but we made it through. I think filing bankruptcy bothered me more than it did Jason. I had reached a point in my life where I prided myself on my high credit score and my practice of always paying my bills on time. It knocked me down for a bit, but it was a good life lesson.

Jason and I began to grow apart. My law enforcement career was going well, and I was trying to learn from the lessons of the past and grow as an individual. I also started taking better care of myself. I quit smoking, cut way back on drinking, and began exercising and eating right. On the other hand, Jason was unhappy with his job and losing the video business. He drank a lot more, didn't quit smoking, and did not take care of himself. He also had some health issues and his doctor told him if he didn't change his diet and start exercising, he would meet an earlier death. You'd think that would have made him change his lifestyle, but Jason continued down the same path. All of this made me feel like Jason was in his own world and I didn't fit in.

The final straw for me was finding a pair of earrings on the headboard that didn't belong to me. When I asked Jason about them, he said he didn't know where they came from and they could possibly belong to his daughter. Let me see. What do I think about that response? *Really? Your daughter's earrings. Do you mean the daughter who doesn't live here, and we see about once every month or two? The daughter who never goes into our bedroom when she does come over? And if she did go into our bedroom, why would she leave her earrings on the headboard of our bed?* Strike three.

Now, here is the part I regret, and I kick myself for it to

this day. I stayed for another year. I couldn't let go of the hope that things could change between us. I was so stupid for ignoring what was staring me in the face. I didn't want to see or feel the betrayal I knew had taken place. I didn't want another failed marriage. But something died in me that day, and so began the crack in the pane of my heart. A breach of the dam that slowly expanded as time went on until there was no more, and I had no choice but to walk away.

## Reflection of Hope

Another failed marriage. Another betrayal. Get married. Get divorced. Rinse. Repeat. Does anyone see a pattern here? I sure didn't, and I don't think I could have recognized it then. I was too busy rinsing and repeating. We get that way sometimes; rinsing and repeating. We keep spinning our wheels even though we've seen the movie at least ten times before, knowing the ending will always be the same. I wouldn't break the pattern until after my next marriage ended. But until then, I was stuck. Unable to change course. Floundering.

I'm not entirely sure why I needed a commitment of marriage, but for some reason, it was vital to me. I'm sure part of it was feeling like I was locking in love. It was a promise. A commitment. It would always be there, which was the assurance I desperately needed. But, out of desperation comes disaster. The desperation felt like being stuck under a layer of ice in a frozen lake and desperately searching for a pocket of air guaranteed to sustain you, at least for a while. The disaster was the inevitable crashing and burning of the relationship.

When you're stuck in the desperate-for-love hamster wheel, it's easy to overlook the warning signs. You see them, but the background is so inviting that you look past them and walk around them to pursue what you think will make you feel happy and whole. You are happy and whole for a while until the danger that the warning signs were trying to tell you about begin to appear, and you can no longer ignore them.

There comes a time when you must find out why you continually ignore the warning signs. It is a time when you have to ask yourself the hard questions and face the demons inside you. No doubt, you have to be ready, and you have to find a safe space in which you can unpack it all and know that when you do, you will come out on the other end a better version of yourself– a much happier version.

It wasn't until I faced my demons that I was in a position to accept the Lord Jesus Christ as my savior. I had to first destroy the demons inside of me and learn to love myself and be honest with myself. Only then was my heart opened to accept Christ Jesus, and I found myself praying for the day the Lord would bring me home. When He did, my search for unwavering love was over.

When the Garden of Eden was closed off to man, so was man's ability to live eternally beside God as he did in the Garden. Jesus lived a blameless life and died a blameless death. Why would He do such a thing? Because He knew the only way to reunite us with God would be to die in our place and use His blood shed through a blameless death as the way to eternal life. Thank you, Jesus!

## Scriptures of Hope

✝ For God so loved the world, that he gave his only begotten Son, that whosoever believeth in him should not perish, but have everlasting life. (John 3:16 KJV).

✝ He who does not love does not know God, for God is love. (1 John 4:8 NKJV).

✝ We love each other because he loved us first. (1 John 4:19 NLT).

✝ See what great love the Father has lavished on us, that we should be called children of God! And that is what we are! The reason the world does not know us is that it did not know him. (1 John 3:1 NIV).

✝ For the grace of God has appeared, bringing salvation for all people, training us to renounce ungodliness and worldly passions, and to live self-controlled, upright, and godly lives in the present age, waiting for our blessed hope, the appearing of the glory of our great God and Savior Jesus Christ, who gave himself for us to redeem us from all lawlessness and to purify for himself a people for his own possession who are zealous for good works. (Titus 2:11-14 ESV).

✝ But God proves his own love for us in that while we were still sinners, Christ died for us. How much more then, since we have now been justified by his blood, will we be saved through him from wrath. For if, while we were enemies, we were reconciled to God through the death of his Son, then how much more, having been reconciled, will we be saved by his life. And not only that, but we also boast in God through our Lord Jesus Christ, through whom we have now received this reconciliation. (Romans 5:8-11 CSB).

✝ In this is love, not that we have loved God, but that He loved us and sent His Son to be the propitiation for our sins. (1 John 4:10 LSB).

✝ I have been crucified with Christ, and it is no longer I who live, but Christ lives in me. So the life I now live in the body, I live because of the faithfulness of the Son of God, who loved me and gave himself for me. (Galatians 2:20 NET).

✝ For I the LORD thy God will hold thy right hand, saying unto thee, Fear not; I will help thee. (Isaiah 41:13 KJV).

✝ The Lord is not slack concerning His promise, as some count slackness, but is longsuffering toward us, not willing that any should perish but that all should come to repentance. (2 Peter 3:9 NKJV).

# Chapter 11

## *Ignoring the Warning Signs*

*All marriages are sacred, but not all are safe.*

— Rob Jackson

I had retired from law enforcement when I met my seventh husband, Ben. I was working in the corporate world and had sworn off men after my divorce from Jason. I wouldn't even date because dating leads to a relationship, and a relationship leads to marriage, and the last thing I wanted to do was to get married again. I made it four years without dating, and then I met Ben.

I purchased a Harley-Davidson Sportster motorcycle and got my motorcycle license when I was 55 years old. I had been a passenger on a motorcycle many times in my life, but I had never had a motorcycle license or driven a motorcycle. I joined the ladies' Harley-Davidson Owners Group (HOG) and was helping put together a HOG breakfast event one Saturday morning. I arrived early and was waiting outside for some of the other ladies to arrive when I saw Ben pull up on his Harley-Davidson Road King motorcycle. That was all it took. I was in love.

Ben and I were practically joined at the hip during the entire breakfast. The mutual attraction was undeniable. When the breakfast was over, Ben asked me if I wanted to go for a ride with him. I hesitated at first, as I had just gotten my motorcycle license and wasn't feeling very confident on my motorcycle yet. On the other hand, Ben had been riding for over forty years and told me we would take it easy. We rode for hours, and by the time we stopped for lunch, I was feeling a lot more comfortable on my bike.

It was during lunch that Ben told me about his ex-girlfriend and how she had been physically abusive to him when they got drunk one night. The night ended with Ben calling the police, which led him to get a protective order against her. The whole story must have freaked him out because as we were getting ready to leave the restaurant he told me he didn't want a serious relationship. That was fine by me. I didn't even want to date. I thought we could be friends and ride together, but despite our mutual opposition to a serious relationship, after about two weeks, we fell in love and were married two months later.

Talk about ignoring the warning signs. I look back and can't believe I married Ben, but I understand why I did. I can't believe I married him because he was controlling, had some drinking issues, and had some serious baggage he was still carrying around from his childhood. I understand why I married him. He was a gentleman; a dying breed. He made me feel like he would always protect me and would never hurt me. That feeling was so strong and hooked into me so deeply that I married Ben after knowing him for two months and knowing it would never last. How did I know it wouldn't last? Once again, I ignored the warning signs, but this time, I was aware of them and chose to ignore them.

## Warning Sign #1

Ben's house was filthy and smelled like cigarette smoke. After his break-up with his girlfriend, Ben didn't really care much about anything and spent most of his spare time playing video games, smoking, and drinking whiskey. I didn't smoke and could hardly stand being in his house. The carpet was dirty and the furniture was in such bad shape that it needed to be thrown out. It was so bad that I don't think a second-hand store would have accepted it. The master bedroom door had a hole in it the size of a softball where Ben's ex-girlfriend had put her fist through it during their drunken fight.

In the spare bedroom there was a small amount of blood spattered on one of the walls, which Ben told me was from his crazy sister, whom he let live with him for a while. Ben said he didn't know how the blood got there. I didn't pry. When it came to cleanliness, Ben and I were complete opposites. I always kept my house clean and organized. Being in his dirty house made me sick. I can't believe I was willing to overlook it. That wasn't the way I lived. But overlook it, I did. Needless to say, Ben moved into my townhouse when we got married and we completely overhauled his house before renting it.

## Warning Sign #2

Ben was controlling from the beginning of the relationship. He was critical of some of the things I wore. He would tell me my dress was too sexy or my shirt was cut too low when, in fact, it wasn't. One time, a girlfriend called me to invite me to her house as she was hosting a luncheon with a few girlfriends. I accepted the invitation, and when I got off the phone, Ben asked me who I was talking to. I told him about the invitation, and he became upset because I didn't ask his permission to attend the luncheon.

Because of Ben, I began isolating myself from friends and family. If I visited a friend or was out with family, Ben would text me every half hour asking me when I was coming home. He wanted me to text him when I arrived anywhere and before I left to come home. When we would go to family gatherings, about thirty minutes after we arrived, Ben would tell me he wanted to leave. I was Ben's whole world, and he wanted to control mine.

## Warning Sign #3

One day, Ben was out in the backyard of his house working on the sprinklers. I commented that a few of the sprinkler heads needed some work. From Ben's reaction to my comment, you would have thought I'd told him he was a worthless bum. He threw a fit and acted like a pouty five-year-old because he said my comment made him feel bad. This was the first of many occurrences when Ben would go off without warning. It got to the point where I felt like I was constantly walking on eggshells because I never knew when the most innocent comment would send Ben into a tailspin.

A short time later, Ben came to me and wanted me to look at the garage he had just organized and cleaned. I went out to the garage and immediately told him what a good job he had done and thanked him for doing it. He noticed he had missed cleaning a shelf and was going into the house to get a rag to clean it. I noticed dirt on the door around the door handle and asked him to grab some spray cleaner while he was getting a rag. Ben returned with the cleaner and a rag and cleaned the shelf he had missed. When he was done, I took the cleaner and rag and cleaned the dirt around the door handle. Ben went off. "Nothing I do is good enough for you, is it?" Ben exclaimed. "I worked on the garage for hours, and all you can do is find a spot I missed. You didn't even thank me for cleaning the garage. Does nothing I do make you happy?"

I never knew how to react when Ben went off like that. I was always so afraid I would say the wrong thing, thinking I was saying the right thing. I would try to make a case for myself, but it just made things worse, and the end result was a shouting match. The next day or hours later, I would apologize to smooth things over. It got to the point where I felt mentally beaten down and was always afraid I would say or do the wrong thing.

## The Abuser Revealed

I remember seeing Ben sweep the kitchen floor, and when he was done, he left the house to go to his shop. I noticed he had missed an area of the floor and thought about whether I should sweep up what he missed. I stood there calculating whether I would have enough time to sweep the area before he came back in the house because I knew if he saw me sweeping the floor he had just swept, there would be hell to pay. I decided I had enough time and began sweeping the area. Before I finished, Ben walked into the kitchen. My heart sank, and I began making excuses as to why I was sweeping the floor, fearing that he would start yelling at me and telling me nothing he did was good enough for me.

Life with Ben was very confusing. On the one hand, he was very supportive of the things I wanted to do, like getting a master's degree and starting a private investigation business. He supported me wholeheartedly in both of these endeavors, but all the while, I felt like I was walking on eggshells emotionally. Never knowing when the powder keg would explode. It was nerve-racking.

This went on for five years. I thought about leaving him numerous times, but I didn't want yet another failed marriage, and for some reason, I still loved him. I taught domestic violence investigation at the police academy where I would tell my students that domestic violence can start out as verbal abuse and then, over the years, escalate to physical abuse. Our relationship was textbook.

Initially, the abuser will shower the victim with attention and make her feel needed and special. Gradually, the abuser will isolate the victim from her friends and family. He would be controlling and make her check in with him when she left the house. He was verbally abusive, which often escalated into physical abuse. This process could take years before the physical abuse would manifest itself.

The great realization for me came when Ben met me for

dinner one night. Ben had been laid off from his job and had difficulty finding another one. He had retirement funds that he had accumulated while he worked, which he needed to move to a different investment firm. I suggested he move the funds to the firm where my investments were and gave him my financial advisor's name and contact information.

It had been several weeks since I had given Ben this information, so while we were having dinner, I asked him if he had been able to contact my financial advisor and have his funds transferred. He said he had spoken with him about it and told me a little about what he said. I asked him some questions, like what type of investment he ended up going with.

Ben lost it and began to raise his voice. "I don't know exactly what kind of an investment it is! Why do you have to be so controlling?"

I was shocked by Ben's response to what I thought was a simple conversation.

"I'm not trying to be controlling. I just asked what type of an investment you decided to go with." I explained.

"I told you I didn't know what it was exactly. You always have to be in control, don't you?" Ben said as he pounded his fist on the table.

The other patrons turned to look at us to see what was going on and watched as Ben yelled at me and pounded his fist on the table hard enough to make the utensils jump. I was so embarrassed, and for the first time, I was afraid of him. Not that I thought he would hurt me in a restaurant, but it was the first time I saw him become even the least bit violent. The light in my head clicked on. Ben had just crossed the line. I grabbed my purse and coat and walked out of the restaurant.

The next morning I was on the fence about whether I should divorce Ben. But Ben decided it for me when he walked into the house and said, "We have a good life."

*What? That's what you have to say after what you did last night? Yes, we have a good life. All of our debts are paid except for the house. You have a gigantic shop and all that you want and need. And, you don't need to work if you don't want to. You mean you have a good life. What about us? I'm not hearing anything like, "I'm sorry I was an idiot last night. I love you. I don't want to lose you. I will do whatever it takes to make this work."*

## The Cycle of Violence

It was then that I realized that I was living the three phases of the cycle of violence that I had been teaching for so many years but was so entrenched in the relationship that I failed to recognize it. The three phases of the cycle of violence are characteristic of abusive relationships, which can take on many forms, such as physical violence, name-calling, public or private humiliation, controlling the victim's actions, threatening to leave, commit suicide, or other negative actions, destroying property or hurting pets, or treating the victim like a servant[1].

The first phase of the cycle of violence is the tension-building phase. This is when the tension starts to build for whatever reason and when the abuser "...begins to assert his or her power over the victim in an attempt to control the victim's actions. Batterers will set rules for the victim that are impossible to follow. They will tell the victim that there will be consequences if they break the rules. Sadly, the consequences usually result in violence against the victim. Rules often may include no contact with family members, money spending rules and/or needing to obtain permission for everything the victim does. Batterers use demeaning, degrading, and derogatory phrases toward the victim in an attempt to "objectify" the victim. This is done because it is easier to commit violence against an "object" rather than someone you are supposed to love.[2]"

The second phase of the cycle of violence has several different names depending on the source. We'll call it the abusive or violent episode, which is the phase when "The tension is too much, and the abuser commits an act of abuse. Abuse may range from physical abuse like hitting to emotional abuse such as name-calling and humiliation. The goal of abuse is always to gain power and control over the victim using any means necessary[3].

The last phase of the cycle of violence is called the honeymoon phase. This phase occurs after the abusive incident and is when the abuser "...usually begins an intense effort to win forgiveness and ensure that the relationship will not break up. Batterers ask for forgiveness, say it will not happen again, and behave in a very loving and kind manner. While batterers apologize, they still blame the victim for the violence, stating, "If you had only stayed home like I asked you, I wouldn't have had to hit you..." or "I'll never do it again..." Often, batterers use gifts to convince the victim to forgive. The victim wants to believe that the abuse will end. The victim's feelings that the abuse will now stop is supported by the batterer's loving behavior[4]."

## Deciding to Jump

The thing about domestic abuse or violence is that once it begins and gains momentum, it continues to increase in severity and frequency. It is a vicious circle that can encapsulate the victim and strip her of her strength and willingness to fight against it or flee from it. Something inside me went dead that night in the restaurant, and I wasn't willing to stick around to see if things would change because I knew they never would. The writing was on the wall.

Now, I'm not saying things would have escalated to domestic violence, but I was definitely living in a version of the three stages of the cycle of violence. That night in the restaurant was my wake-up call. I had never seen that side of Ben before, and it scared me. I had witnessed domestic abuse my entire career in law enforcement and had taught domestic violence investigation classes for many years. I recognized what was happening and felt I was riding a train destined for disaster and needed to jump off the train or be willing to endure the inevitable. I decided to jump.

## Reflection of Hope

Why do females stay when we are in an abusive or potentially violent relationship? According to James Barnett, "While the answer is complex and uncomfortable, the reality is female victims themselves are often attracted and sexually attracted to certain male abuser traits; the 'bad boy,' the heightened machismo, his power and the raw masculinity of his emotions. Loss of emotional control characterizes male abusers, possessiveness, jealousy, insecurity, etc., and female victims often cannot help feeling empathy or love for something supposedly powerful and weak at the same time. This is one of the key reasons why it is so difficult for the female victim to permanently get away from that which may ultimately destroy her[5]."

I was fortunate enough to recognize what was happening in my marriage with Ben and muster the strength to break away from it. There are many reasons why women stay in abusive relationships. The average number of times a woman will leave an abuser before leaving him permanently is seven[6]. Seven times of consciously making a decision to flee from the emotional or physical abuse and actually leaving, only to go back to it again.

It wasn't until my marriage to Ben that I had a personal experience living in this world and had at least some basic understanding of why women go back to an abusive relationship time and time again. If I hadn't seen so much domestic abuse during my law enforcement career and knew so much about it from teaching the subject at the police academy, I am fairly certain I would have stayed. Certainly a lot longer than I did.

I think my age had something to do with my decision to leave Ben. I was sixty-one when I left Ben and didn't want to invest the time I knew it would take to change the landscape of our marriage. But, I was also old enough and had enough experience with domestic abuse that I had the wisdom to recognize it would simply be a huge waste of time and not worth the enormous effort it would take.

Again, the Lord was walking with me and helped me through this troubled time. He kept me from any real danger while I was in the relationship, guided me, and gave me the strength I needed to break away from it. And he did all of this during a time when I was rejecting him. God's love for his children never ceases to amaze me. He didn't have to help me during this time in my life. He could have left me to my destiny of unhappiness and possibly physical abuse, but he didn't.

What kind of a God helps his children when they openly say they want nothing to do with Him and even question His existence? I am now ashamed for having done so. But I have asked for God's forgiveness in this matter, and He has forgiven me through His Son. It's never too late to come home and allow God to love you. You need only ask. "Ask and it will be given to you; seek and you will find; knock and the door will be opened to you. For everyone who asks receives; the one who seeks finds; and to the one who knocks, the door will be opened," (Matthew 7:7-8 NIV). When you ask, you will never feel a greater love than the love you will receive from Him.

## Scriptures of Hope

✝ And I say unto you, Ask, and it shall be given you; seek, and ye shall find; knock, and it shall be opened unto you. For every one that asketh receiveth; and he that seeketh findeth; and to him that knocketh it shall be opened. If a son shall ask bread of any of you that is a father, will he give him a stone? or if he ask a fish, will he for a fish give him a serpent? Or if he shall ask an egg, will he offer him a scorpion? If ye then, being evil, know how to give good gifts unto your children:

how much more shall your heavenly Father give the Holy Spirit to them that ask him? (Luke 11:9-13 KJV).

✝ Through the LORD's mercies we are not consumed, Because His compassions fail not. (Lamentations 3:22 NKJV).

✝ If you make the LORD your refuge, if you make the Most High your shelter, no evil will conquer you; no plague will come near your home. For he will order his angels to protect you wherever you go. They will hold you up with their hands so you won't even hurt your foot on a stone. You will trample upon lions and cobras; you will crush fierce lions and serpents under your feet! The LORD says, "I will rescue those who love me. I will protect those who trust in my name. When they call on me, I will answer; I will be with them in trouble. I will rescue and honor them. I will reward them with a long life and give them my salvation." (Psalm 91:9-16 NLT).

✝ The LORD is compassionate and gracious, slow to anger, abounding in love. He will not always accuse, nor will he harbor his anger forever; he does not treat us as our sins deserve or repay us according to our iniquities. For as high as the heavens are above the earth, so great is his love for those who fear him; as far as the east is from the west, so far has he removed our transgressions from us. As a father has compassion on his children, so the LORD has compassion on those who fear him; for he knows how we are formed, he remembers that we are dust. (Psalm 103:8-14 NIV).

✝ Jesus answered, "Truly, truly, I say to you, unless one is born of water and the Spirit, he cannot enter the kingdom of God. That which is born of the flesh is flesh, and that which is born of the Spirit is spirit. Do not marvel that I said to you, 'You must be born again.' The wind blows where it wishes, and you hear its sound, but you do not know where it comes from or where it goes. So it is with everyone who is born of the Spirit." (John 3:5-8 ESV).

✝ We know that everyone who has been born of God does not sin, but the one who is born of God keeps him, and the evil one does not touch him. We know that we are of God, and the whole world is under the sway of the evil one. And we know that the Son of God has come and has given us understanding so that we may know the true one. We are in the true one — that is, in his Son, Jesus Christ. He is the true God and eternal life. (1 John 5:18-20 CSB).

✝ Jesus Christ is the same yesterday and today and forever. (Hebrews 13:8 LSB).

✝ Free me from prison, that I may give thanks to your name. Because of me the godly will assemble, for you will vindicate me. (Psalm 142:7 NET).

✝ But seek first his kingdom and his righteousness, and all these things shall be yours as well. "Therefore do not be anxious about tomorrow, for tomorrow will be anxious for itself. Let the day's own trouble be sufficient for the day. (Matthew 6:33-34 RSV).

✝ Beloved, let us love one another, for love is from God, and whoever loves has been born of God and knows God. Anyone who does not love does not know God, because God is love. In this the love of God was made manifest among us, that God sent his only Son into the world, so that we might live through him. In this is love, not that we have loved God but that he loved us and sent his Son to be the propitiation for our sins. Beloved, if God so loved us, we also ought to love one another. No one has ever seen God; if we love one another, God abides in us and his love is perfected in us. (1 John 4:7-12 ESV).

# Chapter 12

## *Understanding the Why*

*Your vision will become clear only when you can look into your own heart. Who looks outside, dreams; who looks inside, awakes.*

— Carl Jung

I have taken antidepressants for about twenty-five years and sleep medication for almost fifteen years. I will never be able to function or sleep without them. In April of 2022, I went to see a psychiatrist for a new patient evaluation so she could take over the management of my medications and possibly prescribe something to quell the panic attacks I had been experiencing. She ran me through the gamut of new-patient evaluation questions and then asked, "Besides depression and anxiety, do you think there are any other issues you are dealing with?"

I thought about the question for a minute, and with a confused look, I responded, "No, I can't think of any."

She stopped typing notes on her computer and said, "Let's talk about the elephant in the room. You have PTSD, and I suggest you see a therapist who specializes in treating it."

I couldn't believe what I was hearing and said, "Really? I have PTSD?" She looked at me with raised eyebrows and shook her head affirmatively, indicating it was something that was more than obvious to her.

She explained there is a variation of PTSD called C-PTSD, or complex post-traumatic stress disorder, that can be the result of trauma experienced during childhood. The thought of me having PTSD or C-PTSD never entered my mind. I knew I had a crappy childhood, but was what I experienced trauma? The abortion was traumatizing, but I hadn't told her about that experience. I didn't understand how my psychiatrist was able to settle on a diagnosis of PTSD or C-PTSD, but it was in therapy and through my own research that I was able to understand so many of the whys. Why did I get married seven times? Why did I get pregnant at age thirteen? Why did I get involved with drugs and alcohol?

## EMDR Therapy

Therapy turned out to be life-changing and one of the best experiences of my life. In addition to other techniques, my therapist used a therapy method called EMDR (Eye Movement Desensitization and Reprocessing) that was phenomenally effective and, as I said, was life-changing.

When a normal event occurs in your life, your brain smoothly stores the memory and networks it so it connects to other things you remember. During disturbing or upsetting events, networking doesn't happen correctly. The brain can go "offline," and there's a disconnect between what you experience (feel, hear, see) and what your brain stores in memory through language. Often, your brain stores trauma memories in a way that doesn't allow for healthy healing. Trauma is like a wound that your brain hasn't been allowed to heal. Because it didn't have the chance to heal, your brain didn't receive the message that the danger was over. Newer experiences can link up to earlier trauma experiences and reinforce a negative experience over and over again. That disrupts the links between your senses and memories. It also acts as an injury to your mind. And just like your body is sensitive to pain from an injury, your mind has a higher sensitivity to things you saw, heard, smelled, or felt during a trauma-related event.[1]

EMDR therapy is a mental health treatment technique. This method involves moving your eyes a specific way while you process traumatic memories. EMDR's goal is to help you heal from trauma or other distressing life experiences. When you undergo EMDR, you access memories of a traumatic event in very specific ways. Combined with eye movements and guided instructions, accessing those memories helps you reprocess what you remember from the negative event. That reprocessing helps "repair" the mental injury from that memory. Remembering what happened to you will no longer feel like reliving it, and the related feelings will be much more manageable.[2]

EMDR therapy helps to reprocess tragic and unbearable memories that are frozen in your mind. They are frozen in time and are paralyzing unless they are reprocessed from a different perspective. Through the use of EMDR, I was able to reprocess many traumatic events, such as the abortion and the sexual abuse I experienced. Before EMDR, I blamed myself for the abortion and felt that I was a murderer. I felt that I was a bad person because I allowed it to happen by not refusing to have an abortion. I also resented Alex for wanting me to have an abortion and felt that he didn't love me or our baby.

Through therapy, I realized I wasn't a bad person. This became apparent to me when my therapist asked me, "Would a bad person feel bad about having an abortion?" That's when the light came on. Of course, a bad person wouldn't feel bad about having an abortion! I realized I wasn't a murderer and stopped blaming myself because I knew I didn't want the abortion but felt I had no choice in the matter. I also stopped resenting Alex. I realized that Alex was deathly afraid of the consequences, and even though he loved me, he was terrified of having a child at such a young age. Being able to reprocess having an abortion at a time when I had so much more life experience made it so the memory of the abortion didn't cause me to break down into tears. The sadness remains, but I am better equipped to live with it now.

I wish I would have sought therapy much earlier in my life. Until I underwent mental health therapy and explored my childhood, I couldn't realize how traumatic events had shaped my life by influencing my choices. By not addressing or reprocessing the traumatic memories, you are destined to repeat the self-destructive behavior throughout your life.

## Wiring of the Brain

We all have an innate need to be loved and wanted. Beginning when we are born, our brains begin growing, developing, and weaving a network of neurons according to the type and amount of interaction we experience or don't experience with our parents. Positive and caring interaction with a parent gives a child a sense of being loved, security, and belonging. Conversely, little to no caring interaction with a parent will result in a miswiring of the child's brain, leaving them emotionally damaged.[3]

The most crucial time of the brain's development is the first year of life, which is 90% developed by age three. As the brain grows, a sort of wiring system is formed by experiences and emotions that are exchanged between a parent and the child. The way the brain circuitry is wired is dependent upon what is learned and felt by the child as these exchanges take place. Without a positive and loving exchange between parent and child, the wiring of the brain can be impaired, which can result in learning disabilities and compromised mental health as these children become adults. Adults who experienced this lack of development and miswiring of the brain when they were babies and small children are likely to experience depression, anxiety, learning disabilities, or memory impairments later in life.[4]

My therapist had me take a quiz to determine my attachment style. Attachment styles are patterns of bonding that people learn as children that they carry into their adult relationships. There are four attachment styles:

1. **Secure Attachment:** Securely attached individuals are comfortable with intimacy and can balance dependence and independence in relationships.
2. **Preoccupied Attachment (Anxious in Children)**: Individuals with this attachment style crave intimacy and can be overly dependent and demanding in relationships.
3. **Dismissive Attachment (Avoidant in Children)**: This style is characterized by a strong sense of self-sufficiency, often to the point of appearing detached. Individuals with dismissive attachment value their independence highly and may seem uninterested in close relationships.
4. **Fearful Attachment (Disorganized in Children)**: Individuals with a fearful attachment style desire close relationships and fear vulnerability. They may behave unpredictably in relationships due to their internal conflict between a desire for intimacy and fear of it.[5]

Surprisingly, I have a secure attachment style. My therapist told me this is probably because my biological mother made me feel loved, and because of that, I know how you should make a child feel loved. This is why when I had children, I ensured they knew they were loved daily. Not a day went by that I didn't tell them I loved them and gave them lots of hugs and kisses. I'm grateful for having a mother who made me feel loved, and I know in my heart that if my mother had lived, my childhood would have been the complete opposite of what it was.

## Emotional Neglect and Attachment Injury

Throughout my life, I have made poor decisions and gone down many rocky roads, all in the name of love. For me, the need to be loved was a powerful driving force created by the emotional neglect and attachment injury I experienced as a child.

An attachment injury can be created by a breach of trust in some sort of an interdependent relationship, usually resulting from a specific incident. If left unhealed, feelings of betrayal or abandonment can haunt you later in life[6].

Signs of unprocessed attachment injuries or wounds include feeling anxious in relationships, feeling unfulfilled in most of your relationships, negative self-talk, trust issues, and a history of unhealthy relationships[7].

At the time, neither Brandon nor I could have known the profound effect his teenage curiosity would have on my life. The incident down by the creek with Brandon would lead to the first of many attachment injuries I would experience throughout my childhood. The attachment injuries, coupled with the emotional neglect I experienced from my dad and Brenda, manifested later in my life as an anxiety disorder, depression, trust issues, C-PTSD, a pregnancy at an early age, and a string of unhealthy relationships. For a time, substance abuse was my go-to coping mechanism, which, in many ways, compounded the problem.

According to Ivan Fortune, Child Emotional Neglect

(CEN) refers to a parent's failure to meet their children's emotional needs while growing up. It reflects unresponsive, unavailable, and limited emotional interactions between a parent and the child. Children's needs for emotional care in the form of affection, support, attention, or competence are ignored. Child emotional neglect qualifies as a form of psychological maltreatment. It has been identified as also one of the most prevalent types of childhood abuse. Emotional neglect may not necessarily translate to childhood abuse in the strict sense, considering that abuse is often intentional, that is, a purposeful choice to act in a way that is harmful. Though often not involving traumatic events, experiencing emotional neglect as a child has similar damaging effects as being abused. Some studies even indicate that CEN might have the most wide-ranging negative mental health impact among all childhood maltreatment types. It has strong associations with adverse physical, psychological, and educational outcomes[8].

I found it interesting that the effects of emotional neglect that manifest later in life are different if a mother or a father has emotionally neglected the child. I, of course, drew the short straw in this department, as both of my parents neglected me emotionally.

## Emotional Neglect by a Mother

According to J. L. Anderson, if a child is emotionally neglected by their mother, they can later struggle with abandonment issues. Fear of abandonment can cause relationship breakups and low self-esteem. I've listed below only the symptoms of fear of abandonment that I experienced. Not all of the possible symptoms have been listed.

1. **Rapidly Forming Attachments** - You will reach out to the first person who comes along and feel an intense desire to connect. The problem with this is the people you reach out to are not necessarily the kinds of people you would choose to have in your life if you were thinking more rationally.
2. **Complacency** - Taking great pleasure in fulfilling someone else's needs to the point that you no longer recognize unhealthy relationships or even dangerous ones. You will become whomever you need to be in order to please the other person all because you are afraid that people will leave you if you are not good enough in their eyes.
3. **Extreme Jealousy** - If your emotionally absent mother lavished attention on someone else, you may have experienced feelings of jealousy that you buried down deep inside of you that later reared its ugly head in adult relationships.
4. **Abandoning Relationships** - Fear of rejection can be so strong that you feel the need to be the first to leave a relationship.
5. **Abandonment Depression** - Your self-esteem can plummet whenever you feel alone or afraid. You might feel like you caused your

mother's rejection by not being good enough or interesting enough, which you take out on yourself by isolating yourself or withdrawing from normal activities[9].

## Emotional Neglect of a Daughter by Her Father

According to Jennifer Rio, it has been clearly shown that a girl's development from childhood to adulthood can be hurt by not having a father who cares about her emotionally. In this case, I batted a thousand when it came to the list of struggles daughters of emotionally distant fathers face.

1. **Low Self-Esteem** - Children often blame themselves when their fathers emotionally neglect them, as they don't understand why, and they conjure up a story and assume it's their fault, thinking they are unlovable. Many studies have shown that a father's emotional absence can hurt a girl's sense of self-worth, and if her father neglects her, she can feel less confident in her abilities and value. If a daughter did not have a strong relationship with her father, this can affect her academically, psychologically, professionally, physically, socially, and romantically.
2. **Difficulty in Establishing and Maintaining Healthy Relationships** -

Women with emotionally absent fathers as children often struggle to establish lasting relationships. Since their fathers' neglect left them with emotional scars, they don't want to take a chance of getting hurt again.

3. **Eating Disorders are More Prevalent in Women Whose Fathers are Absent** - Girls who grew up with emotionally absent fathers have a higher chance of suffering from eating disorders and unhealthy obsessions with food or body weight. Also, twice as likely to be obese are daughters who grew up without father figures. Daughters of emotionally distant fathers grow to feel a deep emptiness and insecurity since their desire for a close relationship with their dad is denied. Many daughters ask themselves, "What's wrong with me that my father doesn't love me? Would my father love me more if I had a different body shape or looked differently?"
4. **Suffer From Bouts of Anxiety and Depression** - Girls who had fathers who were emotionally or physically absent as children have a higher likelihood of experiencing anxiety and depression as adults. These women often emotionally isolate themselves out of fear of abandonment and rejection. Since they don't feel worthy and are afraid of being hurt, they avoid healthy love relationships. They might also rush into toxic ones that will inevitably end in heartbreak. In both cases, these women are in

emotional danger and often experience panic attacks and depression. They might never be able to establish meaningful relationships with men if they don't deal with the root of their sadness - an emotionally absent father.

5. **They Are More Likely to be Sexually Active Early** - Teenage pregnancies are less common in girls close to their fathers. When girls with a solid emotional connection with their fathers find a husband, their marriages are more emotionally fulfilling, stable, and long-lasting. Numerous studies have also shown that women who have emotionally or physically absent fathers are more inclined to start having sex earlier and engage in unsafe sexual behaviors. According to studies, homes without a father figure account for more than 70% of teenage pregnancies.
6. **High Risk of Developing an Addiction** - The absence of an emotionally supportive father can trap a girl in a negative loop she can't easily break out of. For this, she might resort to drugs to self-medicate and numb her pain. She is more likely to become entangled in a cycle of substance abuse. Studies have shown that daughters of emotionally distant fathers have a significantly higher chance of abusing drugs and alcohol[10].

Going through therapy was, at times, a very scary road to

go down, but it is a road that changed my life forever. My only regret is that I didn't seek help sooner. A lot of pain and agony could have been avoided. But I guess everything happens when it is supposed to happen. As parents, we must think about how our actions or lack of actions affect our children and the profound influence they can have on them. We must be mindful of the way we are paving for our children and do the best we can to shape them into as whole a person as we possibly can. Love is the key. Love, and lots of hugs and kisses.

# A Final Reflection

*So we have come to know and to believe the love that God has for us. God is love, and whoever abides in love abides in God, and God abides in him.*

— *1* John 4:16 (ESV)

I grew up believing in God. I was baptized in the Lutheran church, went to church on Sundays with my family, attended Sunday school and Vacation Bible School, and attended a parochial school. My stepmother was a bookkeeper for the Lutheran Church and my dad was involved in the church in various capacities. But, everything changed the day Brenda told me I had to get an abortion - It was like the rug of religion was pulled out from under me. I was raised believing abortion was wrong. That if a woman has an abortion, she has sinned. That life begins at conception. But despite our religious beliefs, Brenda chose abortion over public humiliation. Brenda chose herself over me and the life of my child. That was the day I turned my back on God and completely rejected Him.

I would spend the next fifty-plus years rejecting God. I still held the belief that a higher power existed, but I couldn't bring myself to believe in the God I felt had forsaken me and had taken my child from me. It left me feeling angry and alone. It wasn't until I had undergone therapy that I was able to release a lot of my anger and hostility toward my family and God and begin to heal. It was through the healing process that I began to feel God's presence renewed in me.

It began when a long-time friend who is very dear to me told me about a church she had been attending and invited me to go to church with her. She told me about some of the people who attended the church and how friendly and welcoming they had been. I told her it sounded interesting to me and that I might attend a service some day. It was incredible that I would even consider attending a church, as I hadn't stepped foot in a church more than a handful of times over the last fifty or so years. The Holy Spirit was beginning to work in me.

It was at an event my friend was hosting where I met some of the members of her church. They were all so nice and accepting and I could feel the Holy Spirit drawing me toward a renewed relationship with God. The next Sunday I attended a service at my friend's church. Everyone there was very welcoming and after spending some time with them I got the sense that this might be a church I could call home. I continued to attend the church and began longing for the relationship with God that my friend had. I began to pray for that deeper connection with God and after a few weeks, during one of the services at church, I felt the Lord bring me home. It was about four months later that I was baptized and declared my belief of and commitment to the Lord Jesus Christ.

Looking back on my life I realize that even after I rejected God, He never left my side. He was with me and watching over me through the abortion, my drug addiction, my law enforcement career, chemotherapy and all of my marriages. He never stopped loving me. He never gave up on me. He forgave me. And after it was all said and done, he brought me back home to Him.

# Notes

## 2. Love and Death

1. Zavada, Jack. 2020. "The 4 Types of Love in the Bible." Learn Religions. https://www.learnreligions.com/types-of-love-in-the-bible-700177.

## 3. I Died With You

1. "Vacuum aspiration | Surgical Abortion | Treatments." n.d. BPAS. Accessed August 12, 2023. https://www.bpas.org/abortion-care/abortion-treatments/surgical-abortion/vacuum-aspiration/.
2. Ahmad, Saeed. 2022. "The Silent Scream, 1984." YouTube. https://www.youtube.com/watch?v=hstRrYsbffM.
3. Ahmad, Saeed. 2022. "The Silent Scream, 1984." YouTube. https://www.youtube.com/watch?v=hstRrYsbffM.

## 5. Addicted to Love

1. Brewer, Alex, and Kris Gunnars. 2020. "Freebasing: The Same As Smoking Crack? And Other FAQs." Healthline. https://www.healthline.com/health/freebasing#freebase-vs-crack.
2. Erickson, Josh. n.d. "How It's Made - The Kaleidoscope." FlexTrades. Accessed September 18, 2023. https://www.flextrades.com/blog/how-its-made-the-kaleidoscope/.

## 7. Pack Up Your Lip Gloss

1. Corley, Cheryl. 2022. "Increasing women police recruits to 30% could help change departments' culture." NPR. https://www.npr.org/2022/07/31/1111714807/increasing-women-police-recruits-to-30-could-help-change-departments-culture.

## 8. Every Time They Put On The Uniform

1. Ford, Anthony. 2023. "Police Officer Suicide and Suicide Prevention | Danielle Rousseau." Boston University. https://sites.bu.edu/daniellerousseau/2023/02/28/police-officer-suicide-and-suicide-prevention/.

## 11. Ignoring the Warning Signs

1. "Understanding the Cycle of Domestic Abuse." 2018. YWCA South Hampton Roads. https://www.ywca-shr.org/understanding-the-cycle-of-domestic-abuse/.
2. "Domestic Violence: Understanding the Cycle of Violence - LAPD Online." n.d. Los Angeles Police Department. Accessed January 15, 2024. https://www.lapdonline.org/domestic-violence-understanding-the-cycle-of-violence/.
3. "Understanding the Cycle of Domestic Abuse." 2018. YWCA South Hampton Roads. https://www.ywca-shr.org/understanding-the-cycle-of-domestic-abuse/.
4. "Domestic Violence: Understanding the Cycle of Violence - LAPD Online." n.d. Los Angeles Police Department. Accessed January 15, 2024. https://www.lapdonline.org/domestic-violence-understanding-the-cycle-of-violence/.
5. "Why do women go from one abusive relationship to the next?" 2015. LinkedIn. https://www.linkedin.com/pulse/why-do-women-go-from-one-abusive-relationship-next-james-barnett.
6. "Why do women go from one abusive relationship to the next?" 2015. LinkedIn. https://www.linkedin.com/pulse/why-do-women-go-from-one-abusive-relationship-next-james-barnett.

## 12. Understanding the Why

1. "EMDR Therapy: What It Is, Procedure & Effectiveness." 2022. Cleveland Clinic. https://my.clevelandclinic.org/health/treatments/22641-emdr-therapy.
2. "EMDR Therapy: What It Is, Procedure & Effectiveness." 2022. Cleveland Clinic. https://my.clevelandclinic.org/health/treatments/

22641-emdr-therapy.

3. "The importance of early bonding on the long-term mental health and resilience of children." 2016. NCBI. https://www.ncbi.nlm.nih.gov/pmc/articles/PMC5330336/.
4. "The importance of early bonding on the long-term mental health and resilience of children." 2016. NCBI. https://www.ncbi.nlm.nih.gov/pmc/articles/PMC5330336/.
5. Huang, Stephanie. 2024. "Attachment Styles In Relationships." Simply Psychology. https://www.simplypsychology.org/attachment-styles.html.
6. "Overcome attachment injury and move forward stronger." 2020. HPRC-online.org. https://www.hprc-online.org/social-fitness/relationship-building/overcome-attachment-injury-and-move-forward-stronger.
7. LeQuang, Natalie. 2017. "10 Signs of Unprocessed Attachment Wounds — Safe Haven Trauma Services, PLLC - Nashville, TN." Safe Haven Trauma Services. http://safehaventherapy.com/blog/2017/8/6/10-signs-of-unprocessed-attachment-wounds.
8. Fortune, Ivan. 2022. *How to Achieve Sanity From Childhood Emotional Neglect.*
9. Anderson, J. L. 2014. *The Emotionally Absent Mother*. 3rd ed.
10. Rio, Jennifer. n.d. *Healing for Daughters of Emotionally Absent Fathers.*

# About the Author

Terry Lotus is a twenty-year law enforcement veteran who served at local, state and federal law enforcement agencies. Her experience with childhood abuse, abortion, and domestic abuse in her own life positions her to bring a powerful message to women and law enforcement officers everywhere, with a reminder that no matter how dark the circumstances or deep the pain, there is always hope.